"If you want an inspir[ing story of a man] who has his heart set u[pon serving God], no matter the cost, you must read *His Faithfulness Reaches to the Skies*. As a missionary pilot in several South American countries, Forrest Zander replays the joys, sorrows, and unique challenges of aviation in the Amazon jungle. His stories warm the heart and build conviction. Read with caution—for God may use it to challenge you to invest your life in the unmet need of this lost world."
J. Paul Nyquist, Ph.D., President, Moody Bible Institute

"Need a faith lift? If you're inspired by true stories of God showing up in the lives of real men and women, you won't want to miss *His Faithfulness Reaches to the Skies* by Forrest Zander. Engine failure at 7,000 feet over South American jungle with no place to land? Cancer? Friends mistaken for drug smugglers and jailed in a foreign country? In these situations and many more, God demonstrates His love for His children. A great read for yourself—a perfect gift for a friend."
Bernie May, Former President of JAARS, Former President of Wycliffe, Founder of The Seed Company

"The Old Testament tells of God's specific preparation, gifting and selection of Bezalel to build the Tabernacle. Forrest Zander's book shows such action by God wasn't just some thousands of years ago story but is repeated today right in our midst. As a friend and colleague of Forrey for over 40 years I assure you that you are meeting the real Forrey in this book, fun loving, yet serious about his life with Jesus and with an in-

fectious love for God, His Word and the people God brings into his life, wherever they are! This fast moving book will both reassure and challenge you in your walk with God."
Martin Huyett, Executive Director, Aramaic Bible Translation

"Many years ago I learned that missionaries, far from being the rejects who couldn't cut it in America, are the brightest, some of the most creative and passionate of God's people. This realization has marked my own sense of calling and mission, for which I shall be forever grateful. As I have read and heard their accounts, the words from Hebrews 11:38, '...of whom the world was not worthy,' have often come to mind.
"Forrest and Margaret have been great friends for many years. It has been especially enjoyable to be teamed with them in various Bible and missionary conference settings. Forrey loves to display his skill with the blowgun, shooting at balloons attached to a board—and promising to shoot one off Burt's head. I'm so glad that he is indeed a good shot—if you get the point!
"*His Faithfulness Reaches to the Skies* is a significant read. You will laugh at times and weep at times. Throughout, you will see God's faithfulness to the Zanders as well as their faithfulness to God's call upon their lives. It will also send you to your knees asking God to work in your own heart."
Rev. Burt Kettinger, Sound Servant Ministries

"A great example of a servant totally committed to the Lord. It will make you cry and laugh and you will find it hard to put the book down."
Bill Dillon, Founder & President Inner City Impact, Founder & President People Raising

"In *His Faithfulness Reaches to the Skies*, Forrey Zander puts readers in the co-pilot's seat for one of the most harrowing—and important—jobs in all of missions: that of the aviators who transport people, food and supplies into and out of the most remote and dangerous places on earth. His thrilling stories will inspire readers to put their own gifts and interests to use in fulfilling the Great Commission."
Bob Creson, President/CEO, Wycliffe USA

"A penetrating examination of a critical sphere of Christian mission by one of its most illustrious practitioners. This book will provide you with vision and practical tools for strengthening your own mission in the world."
Rev. Dr. Daniel D. Meyer

"Forrest Zander writes as he has lived—passionately for Jesus Christ. What a book, what an adventure, what a life, what a Savior!!! *His Faithfulness Reaches to the Skies* is a captivating account of God's redemptive work in and through a man, a couple, a family and a mission agency sold out to the Lord and His kingdom purposes. It compels us to 'Go and make disciples of

all nations' to the utter most parts of the earth. God's faithfulness is unfolded for us throughout the remarkable ministry of Forrest and Margret Zander with Wycliffe Bible Translators. How reassuring to read of God's sovereignty and compassion in all areas of life, even in the tragic loss of a child and spouse. The goodness of God continues to be evident by bringing Wanda into Forrest's life to enable them to serve the Lord together. It's a great read."
Pastor Paul Jorden, Bethel Community Church

"I have read many books in my time—more than I care to remember—but none quite like this. Here is a book that tells a story, a story with honesty and grace, about the life well lived. A life lived for Christ as a missionary pilot. If you love missions, you will love this book. And in it you will find the secret of that life well lived: give it all to Jesus."
Josh Moody, Senior Pastor, College Church in Wheaton

Forrest Zander

His Faithfulness Reaches to the Skies:
The story of a missionary pilot

Forrest Zander
with Dwight Clough

Copyright © 2015 Forrest Zander
All rights reserved.

Cover design by Hans Clough (HansClough.com)
"Your faithfulness reaches to the skies." Psalm 36:5 NASB

Bible translations used herein include
NIV: THE HOLY BIBLE, NEW INTERNATIONAL VERSION®, NIV® Copyright © 1973, 1978, 1984, 2011 by Biblica, Inc.® Used by permission. All rights reserved worldwide.
MEV: Scripture taken from the Modern English Version. Copyright © 2014 by Military Bible Association. Used by permission. All rights reserved.
NASB: Scripture taken from the NEW AMERICAN STANDARD BIBLE®, Copyright © 1960, 1962, 1963, 1968, 1971, 1972, 1973, 1975, 1977, 1995 by The Lockman Foundation. Used by permission.
KJV: King James Version: Public domain.

While the stories herein are true, in places the details of the narrative have been changed slightly to protect the privacy of some individuals and/or to help with the flow of the story.

His Faithfulness Reaches to the Skies

"When I grow up, I want to be a pilot because it's a fun job and easy to do. That's why there are so many pilots flying around. Pilots don't need much school. They just have to read numbers so they can read their instruments. I guess they should be able to read road maps too so they can find their way if they get lost. Pilots should be brave so they won't get scared if it's foggy and they can't see or if a wing or a motor falls off they should stay calm so they will know what to do. Pilots have to have good eyes to see through the clouds and they can't be afraid of thunder and lightning because they are so much closer to them than we are. The salary pilots make is another thing I like. They make more money than they know what to do with. This is because most people think that plane flying is dangerous except pilots don't because they know how easy it is. I hope I don't get air sick because because I get car sick and if I get air sick I couldn't be a pilot and then I would have to go to work."

Written by a 5th grader

Reprinted with permission from *Air Line Pilot* magazine.

Forrest Zander

DEDICATION

In loving memory of my wife, sweetheart, and ministry partner, Margaret Marie Morgan Zander, in recognition of her faithful service to the Lord and her prayers for me, our children, our grandchildren, other family members, our missionary colleagues, and our friends. She was promoted to Glory unexpectedly and quickly in 2013.

To my children, Anita (Tim), Arlene (Randy), Alby (Lorri), and my grandchildren, Nora Margaret, Charles Forrest, Zachary Newton, Mattelin Morgan, Leeya Lorraine, Colbey Morgan, Samson Parker, and Benjamin Peda. They are the inspiration and motivation for writing this book. I want them to see God's faithfulness to their mother/grandmother and me throughout our lifetimes.

To my missionary colleagues, my heroes with whom we labored over the years, to provide the Word of God in mother tongues in many languages in South America and throughout the world.

To our family members, devoted friends, and churches who have supported us over the years with their faithful prayers and financial support.

To my wonderful wife, Wanda Jean Zander, for her encouragement and valuable assistance in writing this book.

His Faithfulness Reaches to the Skies

PREFACE

The early makings of this book began when my beloved wife, Margaret, wrote to her mother while in Bible school in Canada. Her letters to her mother continued when she joined Wycliffe Bible Translators, went to Jungle Training in Mexico, and during various assignments in the Mexico Branch of Wycliffe. After Margaret and I were married, I became part of her letters. She wrote regularly during our years in Peru, Ecuador, and Colombia, sharing everyday experiences of missionary life. The letters were written on a typewriter with an original and several copies using carbon paper. These copies were then mailed to her mother in Oregon, my parents in Illinois, and our siblings scattered about the country. When her mother passed away, we attended her funeral and then gathered a few possessions. Among them we discovered a cardboard box in which Mother Morgan had saved perhaps every letter ever received from her daughter Margaret. Most were in their original envelopes with stamps representing the various countries from which they were mailed. This box became a huge treasure, documenting many of our experiences, almost like a journal, or today's blogs. They helped me remember some of the incidents in this book which I had forgotten. Others I only recently learned about because I was off flying somewhere when they occurred.

The actual writing of this book began back in 2002 when Dwight Clough interviewed me for a book he and Tom Shaw were writing for the Moody Bible Institute Alumni Association. At the time it was thought that book would consist of brief biographies of several Moody Alumni. Later it was shortened to 15 stories about alumni of whom I was one. Fortunately Dwight saved the material from the longer interview. He mentioned at the time that if I ever wanted to write a book, he would be glad to assist me. During the intervening years, I was writing stories of my flying experiences in the jungles of Peru, Ecuador, and Colombia, hoping each would become a chapter in any book I might write.

In 2014, I contacted Dwight for help in putting this book together. By that time, my wife Margaret had passed away, and I had married again. My wife, Wanda, became a major contributor and encourager, organizing the letters in folders by year, editing some of the stories, and doing the final read-through before submitting it to Dwight for the finishing touches.

In the early stages, Wanda and I drove to Sun Prairie, Wisconsin, and met with Dwight. We enjoyed a lovely lunch served to us by his gracious wife, Kim, and met some of their children at the table. At Dwight's request, I told the family some of the stories that are in this book and answered their questions.

During our conversations that day, Dwight asked me why I was writing the book. I told him that first, I wanted my children and grandchildren to know what Margaret and I had done as we served together in ministry. But the main purpose would be to demonstrate to God's people and the world the faithfulness of our God and Savior throughout our lifetimes. Truly His faithfulness reaches to the skies!

His Faithfulness Reaches to the Skies

Our prayer is that you, the reader, will be encouraged and will glorify our Lord Jesus as you see His faithfulness demonstrated throughout the book.

Forrest Zander

January, 2015

Table of Contents

PREFACE	8
1. GOD HAD A PLAN	16
Flying with danger	16
Miracle baby	20
A blind woman opened my eyes	21
Overcoming doubt	21
A dilemma	22
A solution	23
The dean's prophetic words	23
Getting into Moody Bible Institute	24
Adventures in flight training	24
Another hurdle—public speaking	28
A gift from above	29
Married in Mexico	34
Heading to the mission field	36
Language study	37
2. LIFE AS A MISSIONARY PILOT	42
Stranded!	42
"Hazel" and the corn flakes	45
Cargo	46
Fuel	50

A very scared passenger	51
Unexpected ministry opportunities	54
Expecting our first child, Forrest Jr.	55
A tragic loss	55
God never makes a mistake	58
Names	59
Anna Marie's birth	60
Tree frog	62
Army ants	63
Having fun	63
Gator hunting	64
Fishing	66
Communication via ham radio	67
Anita's first birthday	68
3. AMAZING TRANSFORMATION	70
Former murderers become friends	70
An airstrip for the Waorani (Auca)	74
Quick thinking	76
Meeting the Waorani (Auca) people	77
Hunting and fishing with the Waorani	81
Anita visits the Waorani	83
The president's visit	84
Full circle	87
The need for Bible translation	89

4. FLYING IN COLOMBIA — 91

- A door opens in Colombia — 91
- Met at gunpoint — 93
- Provision from the sky — 100
- A narrow escape — 104
- No oil pressure — 107
- Engine stops at 7,000 feet — 108
- No brakes! — 109
- The "in house" — 110
- Who is this Jesus? — 111
- The Cuiba — 114
- Snakes — 117
- Stung! — 118
- Running out of fuel — 120
- Trouble at 4,000 feet — 122
- No airstrip—no problem — 125
- Whoops, wrong country! — 127
- Capitán Fori — 128
- Malaria — 129
- A near disaster — 129
- Saved by the storm — 131
- A successful hunt — 134
- Banana trees, flying ants, and a new member in "The Family" — 136
- A badly burned baby — 141

An Indian wedding	143
Anita's mysterious illness and recovery	145
Flying safely	148
Crossing the cultural divide	151
More heroes and Christmas 1968	152
The Paez people	157
Treated by a witch doctor	159
The fire	161
Growing up in Colombia: My children share their memories	162
Surviving a near crash landing	165
What happened to Ron	167
5. DIPLOMACY	170
Missionaries in jail	170
Standing before the president	174
The bomb	175
"You must leave the country!"	176
Behind the scenes with Uncle Cam	186
Wonderful hostess	189
6. RETURNING HOME	191
The road back home	191
A window into Margaret's heart	192
Fishing for men	193
Cancer	195

Jesus	196
Lessons from Old Testament kings	197
Still seeking the lost	198
Margaret's passing	199
Anita's letter to her mom	201
A letter to family and friends	203
Letter from Wanda	207
Colombia	209
Looking ahead	210
Our family	212
About the authors	217
The glory goes to God	218

Chapter 1

GOD HAD A PLAN

Flying with danger

1964-1969

For years I worked as a missionary pilot flying passengers, medicine, and other cargo in and out of some of the most challenging airstrips in the world. The terrain was rugged. Our airstrips were primitive. And flying conditions were far from ideal.

One of the airstrips, in the foothills of the Andes Mountains, was nothing more than a pasture on the side of a mountain at 3500-foot elevation. The airstrip itself cried danger. Airstrip—a poor choice of word. Better to call it "A Disaster Waiting to Happen." Located in the foothills of the Andes, in the shadows of 16,000-foot peaks, it gave an illusion of normality. Until you tried to land. Or take off.

The runway—if you could call it that—was little more than a 400-foot mountain path. Landing was like flying straight into the side of a hill. Even though we had the best airplane for the conditions, a high-performance Helio Courier, the surrounding rugged terrain prevented us from making a normal approach. Once we committed to landing, there was no turning back. We had no choice but to thrust our plane into the bottom of the slope, then use full power to climb to the top. It was so steep you could hardly taxi uphill after landing. At the top of the hill we unloaded our passengers and cargo.

Takeoff down the hill made my heart pound. It was like riding a giant roller coaster, with no room for error. The slightest mistake would send the plane, my passengers, and me into the trees on either side or crashing into the hills just beyond the airstrip. Once started, I had to break ground quickly, avoid a tree on either side, and then climb over a steep ridge. There the terrain fell vertically about 500 feet to a narrow river canyon. Engine failure on takeoff assured a crash, which would probably be fatal.

The first time I flew to that area, Uncle Cam[1] said, "You must land there, because those missionaries (Bible translators, Paul and Edna Headland, working among the Tunebo Indians) have a three-day mule trip in order to get there from the nearest airstrip. You need to land and provide air service for them."

He was twisting my arm, but I could see his point. Here was a choice between a twelve-minute flight and a three-day mule trip. He wanted me to land, come what may. But I didn't want to commit myself until I had a chance to see it. I said, "Uncle Cam, I will fly over the airstrip and, at that time, I will make my decision as to whether it is safe to land or not."

I landed. And, as time passed, I made sure other pilots were qualified to land under these conditions.

One time, I checked out Ron, a new pilot, to make sure he

---
1 Cameron Townsend, founder of Wycliffe Bible Translators

could operate to and from this landing field. Ron did very well. So I remained behind at the big airstrip, while Ron shuttled in the missionaries and their cargo. This required more than one trip because the missionaries planned to stay at this remote site for several weeks. But there were some time constraints. As a rule, we needed to finish by ten o'clock in the morning before contrary winds made takeoff and landing dangerous or impossible.

Ron left on his first shuttle flight about 8:30 AM. He had a 24-minute round trip plus unloading, so within 45 minutes he should have been back. I waited. Ten o'clock rolled around; he wasn't back. Eleven o'clock. Twelve o'clock. All the while I was looking at my watch wondering, "What's happened to Ron?"

I didn't have a radio with me, so I had no way of knowing if Ron was safe or in trouble, dead or alive. I could picture in my mind each scenario. He could have landed short and crashed into the hill just before touchdown. Or if he landed too long, he would have gone over the cliff on the other side. If he attempted to abort landing and made a go-around, the plane couldn't outclimb the terrain. He would crash into the mountainside. The winds picked up mid-morning and added to the danger. Crosswinds. Tailwinds. Maybe we should have quit earlier and finished tomorrow.

All I could do was wait and pray. One o'clock. Two o'clock. Three o'clock. No sign of Ron…

Translators' wood burning stove weighing 150 lbs. delivered by air, carried for two hours over difficult terrain to their village by Tunebo man.

First landing on newly constructed jungle airstrip. It is one-way in and then turn around for takeoff.

Miracle baby

1935

My story begins three decades earlier in the middle of the Great Depression.

After my parents married in the early 1930s, they wanted to start their family right away, but medical science told them their dream was impossible. They would never have children.

But the Bible says that God settles the childless woman in her home as the happy mother of children (Psalm 113:9 NIV). So my parents appealed to their Father in heaven. Like Hannah and Elkanah in the Old Testament (1 Samuel 1), they prayed. And when they learned that a child was on the way, they dedicated me to the Lord before I was born. After my birth in 1935, my parents publicly set me apart for the Lord in a dedication service at a little mission church in rural Chicago Heights, Illinois.

From the top l. to r. Doreen Betty, William John, Beverly Joyce, Forrest Gene

And just as the Lord blessed Hannah with other children after Samuel was born, so also the Lord gave my parents another son and two daughters.

Forrest Zander

A blind woman opened my eyes

1942

We were a church-going family. Sunday School was part of growing up. In our church, the Primary Department Sunday School Superintendent was blind. But she opened my eyes to the truth of the gospel. At the time, I was only six and a half, but I already knew the awful truth about hell, and it scared the wits out of me. When the Sunday School Superintendent invited us to come forward to receive Jesus Christ and His forgiveness, I was ready. I invited Jesus into my heart, went home, and told my mom about my decision.

She smiled and said, "Well, now that you're saved, here's a scissors. You can cut out the handwork for my Sunday School class for next Sunday." Within an hour of accepting the Lord, I was already starting to serve.

Overcoming doubt

ca. 1945

Like many people, I went through a season of doubt. I wrestled with questions like: *Is there really a God? How can I be saved if I'm questioning God's existence?*

These doubts came to a head one night. I became so unsettled that I said to my mom, "You know, I'm not sure I'm saved."

She replied, "If you're not sure, you bow down right here, and you tell that to the Lord."

So I prayed, "If I've never been saved before, save me now."

At that moment, the Lord brought a huge sense of peace and well-being into my life.

A dilemma

1943

When I was seven or eight years old, Vaughn Shoemaker, a cartoonist for the Chicago Tribune, visited our church. I sat on the front row listening to every word. Mr. Shoemaker said, "Now, some of you have already received the Lord, and you've given Him your heart. But, did you know that the Lord wants your whole life? If you'd like to give your whole life to the Lord, I'd like to see your hand."

I can remember that moment as though it were yesterday. It was as if the Lord were raising my hand. My will and His were together. At this tender age, I gave my life wholly to the Lord.

But there was a problem. I was painfully shy.

Mr. Shoemaker said, "If you've responded to the invitation tonight, I'd like you to come down to the lower level of the church. I want to talk to you."

I walked down the stairs, but when I opened the door, there sat fifty people, listening to Mr. Shoemaker's counsel. That was too much. There was no way I was going to walk into a room of fifty people. I turned around and wandered around the church that night, while the rest of those people were counseled.

Being shy created a real dilemma for me as I was growing up. I knew I would be serving God. But the only way I knew to do that was to get up in front of a crowd as a pastor and preach. I could barely handle one-on-one conversations, much less a whole roomful of people. *How can I ever be a preacher? I'm scared to death of people.*

A solution

1950-1951

God showed me the solution to my dilemma when I was a sophomore in high school. I saw a film produced by Moody Bible Institute and Wycliffe Bible Translators that showed the graduates of Moody aviation training program flying airplanes and serving God as pilots and mechanics in Peru, South America.

Here it was! An opportunity to serve God that didn't involve public speaking. God had a place for shy people!

After that service, I went home and told my parents, "I think I would like to be a missionary pilot."

The dean's prophetic words

1950-1951

The very next Saturday, on my dad's next day off work, he drove me to Moody Bible Institute in downtown Chicago. We met Dean Ralph Snow, sat through some classes, and drove out to Wooddale, Illinois, where the flight training program was located at that time.

But before we left the downtown campus, Dean Snow said something to me that proved to be prophetic.

"Forrest," he said, "if you become a missionary pilot, you may stand before presidents and kings and represent the Lord."

Wow! That thought replayed itself many times in my mind, and years later it actually came true.

Getting into Moody Bible Institute

1953

Getting into Moody's flight training program was no easy task. Two to three hundred applicants vied for twelve open slots.

I started to pray and to work hard. I took every high school course I could that might be relevant, from mechanics to advanced math. I studied hard and qualified for the National Honor Society.

I did my best, and then prayed, "Lord, if you want me to study at Moody to be a missionary pilot, I have to get in." In May of my senior year, the letter arrived. "Congratulations," it read, "you have been accepted." That was one of the highlights of my life.

Adventures in flight training

1953-1957

Lives depended on the training pilots received at Moody. Most pilots would never land or take off on the airstrips that we flew in and out of every day on the mission field. A poorly trained pilot would never survive. To this day, I appreciate the professional, technical training that we received. From aviation to mechanics, our instructors modeled the godly life we hoped to live and built professionalism into all of our work. Bible, theology, and missions courses rounded out the well-planned curriculum.

As I was approaching the approximately 40-50 hours of flying experience required for a Private Pilot license, one goal was to complete the cross country requirement. One bright but very cold winter day, I departed Moody-Wooddale Airport west of Chicago to navigate to and land at a distant airport about 50 miles from Moody-Wooddale. Upon landing, I found someone at the airport office, an operator or employee, to sign and date my logbook. I taxied for takeoff on the snowy runway to return home. Pre-takeoff check complete, I began my takeoff run and then commenced the climb out. Suddenly the engine began to falter. Remembering the instructors' emphasis on the possibility of carburetor ice that could cause the engine to quit, I quickly pulled the carburetor heat control. To my surprise, I heard pieces of ice clinking as they left the carburetor. They quickly melted and, sure enough, the engine roared back to life. I was learning to apply basic procedures early in my flying career that would later keep me alive in mission field conditions. I also learned how the Lord graciously guides and protects me as I trust in Him.

Another aspect of training involved getting a checkout in various types of aircraft. Our primary trainer was a Piper J-3 Cub. But we also got experience in the Aeronca Champion and Luscomb. When I was ready for my Commercial license test, I did it in the Aeronca. By that time I knew the aircraft so well that it fit like a glove. I could land it on a dime. I passed with "flying" colors.

A missionary pilot came to Moody with Wycliffe's first Helio Courier, "City of Chicago." We all got a ride in it. Little did I know that I would someday be flying that very same aircraft in Ecuador. (See photo, page 62.)

During my second year at Moody, I was invited during Christmas vacation to fly to Florida with a fellow classmate. We planned to stop in Alabama for a visit with my roommate, Delmar Peterson, a Christian Education major. He was home for vacation with his family; his father pastored a church in Silver Hill. We had hoped to make it from Chicago to Silver Hill in one day, but the early winter nightfall forced us to land in northern Alabama. It was a balmy 60 degrees when we arrived. Not aware of how the mercury drops once the sun sets, we slept under the wing. The overnight temperature bottomed out at about 20 degrees. Even with sleeping bags and winter coats wrapped around us, we still nearly froze to death.

Our trip took us on to Florida for warmer climes, orange juice, and more adventure. We were fascinated with the number of ex-military airports, built during World War II, that were converted to city or regional airports. Our trip took us through Mississippi, Georgia, northern and central Florida, on to Miami, and eventually to Key West. Wow!

Returning via the Gulf coast, we encountered bad weather with low clouds and rain. The airport operator in the South (Naples) told us not to delay, that we could land on almost any stretch of sandy beach all the way to central Florida. When we got to Venice, we would see the airport with one of the runways that started right at the beach. A right turn put us in position for landing. Flying just above the beach, we enjoyed improving weather and gained valuable time. We landed on the beach anyway, just to gain the experience. We picked up sea shells and other beach artifacts, including a coconut, and then continued north.

Our aircraft cruised at about 85 mph. During our return flight north we ran into a cold front with strong northerly headwinds. Our ground speed was reduced to 40 mph. Looking down, we watched the cars on the highway pass us! We only made it to Tennessee that day and needed another day to get home. But as we followed the Illinois Central Railroad and got to central Indiana in bad weather, it began to rain. Suddenly the windshield iced over and we could not see ahead. If we continued, the wings might ice up and cause us to crash. We read about this danger in books and talked about it in class, but now it was real life. New experience! We found an airport close to the railroad but how do you land when you can't see ahead? I flew as best I could looking out the side windows, made the approach in a crab allowing us to see the runway from the side, and then at the last second straightened out our landing run and touched down. It was a huge feeling of relief to be on the ground. The airport operator was a former Moody student who greeted us warmly.

As our training continued, we learned about night flying, seaplanes, instrument flying, and more cross-country flights. We did a long-distance cross-country flight to southern California that included mountain experience. The Lord was building into my life much of what I would need to safely fly on the mission field. But I kept dreaming about the day when I would be there and actually do it!

Another hurdle—public speaking

When I was growing up, I was deathly afraid of public speaking. I became a missionary pilot partly because I didn't think I would have to speak or preach in public. But things came around full circle.

Losing my fear of public speaking was gradual. Each time I had to do it, it was easier. When I was a Moody student, my pastor asked me to speak at an evening service, to bring the sermon or message. That was a biggie and helped a lot. In addition, once I realized I needed to speak to inform God's people of my calling and to raise support, I was thrust into it. I wanted to get to the mission field so this was part of the process. When I first started at Moody, a friend there sold me his slide camera, and I started documenting my life as an aviation student. We put together a slide presentation about our Moody training to share in churches. I turned it into a life story which continued in each phase: Moody, Mexico, Jungle Camp, marriage, getting ready to go to the field, Spanish study—each of these became a series of stories that I still use today.

During my years in Wycliffe, a Dale Carnegie expert taught me how to perfect my presentations before a live audience. Now I stand before hundreds of people and speak. Sure, I can still get nervous if I think about it, but as soon as I get up in front, the nervousness leaves, and I know I'm where I should be.

A gift from above

1958

Moody gave me everything I needed and wanted to get established as a missionary pilot. Well, almost everything. One thing was still lacking.

Many people find their life's partner in Bible college, but I did not. Although there were fine Christian young women at Moody, I did not meet the right person with the same commitment to missions that I had. I knew if I developed a relationship with the wrong woman, I could be easily derailed and miss my life's calling. So I made a decision. If I had to go single, I was willing to go single. I left the matter with the Lord, packed single sheets, single pillowcases, and set out.

What I didn't know was this: the Lord had someone waiting for me.

My first stop was jungle training in Mexico. I flew from Chicago to Mexico City. A kind retired gentleman met me at the Mexico City International Airport, helped me through customs, and took me to the Wycliffe guest house called "The Kettle." I was terribly thirsty and found my way to the kitchen to ask for a drink. There was Margaret Morgan, helping a translator's wife prepare canned meat to take to their village. I didn't know her, and it didn't occur to me that she might someday be my wife. The next day at breakfast she entered the room and I noticed that she was very attractive.

But she had a baby in each arm. I thought, *She's the only good-looking woman I've seen around here, but she's taken.* Only later did I learn that she had been babysitting, and that she was single. But the task before me was to get to southern Mexico for Jungle Camp. All thirty-five of us new recruits were put on a bus for the twenty-four hour journey through beautiful mountains, desert, and finally the end of the road in Chiapas State. Then a missionary pilot flew us, 3 at a time, on a 45 minute flight to a beautiful jungle valley called Yah-sho-quin-te-la, the site of the first phase of jungle training.

The purpose was to prepare us for primitive living: how to maintain our spiritual life, lose our fear of the unknown, and enjoy, or at least cope, without the normal comforts of life in the USA. The first six weeks were called Main Base: living in thatch-roofed cabins with mud walls and floors, cooking on a wood stove, with classes in survival should we get lost in the jungle. Basic medicine, handling a dugout canoe on a jungle river, rustic carpentry, meal preparation, swimming, hiking to build up our physical endurance, and visiting local Indian villages to learn some of the their culture gave us confidence to handle situations we would face on the mission field.

I didn't know how to swim and only did a kind of dog paddle to keep my head above water. Swim class was excellent training. Learning all the basic strokes and swimming against the current, going a bit farther each day to stretch my endurance, I ended up a good swimmer. Weekend hikes of increasing duration built our endurance and put us in excellent physical shape.

The second six weeks, Advanced Base, was located over a mountain range requiring us to hike those twenty-five miles, cook for the group of 35 trainees, and sleep in jungle hammocks on the trail. When we arrived, we were divided into teams of two single men, two single women, or a married family unit, some with children.

Our first task was to build a small hut (champa in the local language), gathering materials from the jungle and using palm leaves that grew along the river for the roof. We were issued rations for each set of two weeks and expected to make it to the next issue. My teammate, Arlo Heinrichs, and I went to work on our Champa. Being ravenously hungry after the long hike, according to instructions, we built our mud stove. Within three days, we had consumed our entire two-week issue of food. We sought out the instructor and requested more food. Her answer: "Sorry, you will have to learn to trust the Lord."

One of the requirements was to make a village visit as a team. Arlo and I hiked as soon as possible to the nearest village and negotiated enough food to last us until the next issue. We also began fishing in the Jatate River flowing beside our Champa. We caught enough fish to feed ourselves and several other campers. We thoroughly enjoyed the experience and gained confidence in our ability to live off the land.

In another part of our survival training, half of us were taken into the jungle to survive a simulated plane crash. The other half played the role of rescuers. I was in the "crash" group. We were allowed minimum equipment—a military canteen, matches, fish hooks and line, water purification tablets and a machete. As part of my two-man team, I gathered clams from the river to cook in my canteen cup. I caught a small five-inch fish. Not much meat on that critter! We found some wild pineapple—small but providing some nourishment. We slept in the jungle without hammocks or other bedding. Most of all we learned to trust the Lord. During that time, Psalm 37:3-7 became especially meaningful to me. "Delight yourself in the Lord, and He will give you the desires of your heart." (Psalm 37:4 MEV) They continue to be some of my favorite verses. Soon the rescue party found us and returned us to camp.

As the end of Advanced Base approached, we were divided into groups of six, issued instructions, and required to build a balsa wood raft. It had to be big and sturdy enough to carry six people (plus duffel bags) twenty-five miles downstream to the nearest airstrip. Then we were flown back to civilization and, having survived Jungle Camp, we thought of ourselves as "real missionaries."

After the three months in jungle training, I was asked to stay an extra six weeks in Mexico to be the maintenance man at the translation center in Mitla, Oaxaca. The next time I met Margaret Morgan, she was teaching missionary kids at this very same Wycliffe Bible Translators center where I was assigned.

The meal arrangement for me was to eat breakfast with one translator family, lunch with a different family, and the evening meal with four single missionary girls at their apartment. I will never know if I was "set-up," but I did get to know them, and particularly Margaret. When it was her turn to cook, I found out that she was really good at it. I stayed those evenings to dry dishes as she washed them, and the Lord began to knit our hearts together.

Margaret came to watch the volleyball games in which we missionary men played against the local Mexicans. She and I took walks, but always with one or two of the school kids that Margaret was teaching. We were warned not to be alone in order to observe the local cultural norms. By the end of the six weeks, I was smitten and left my heart with her.

When I returned to my home in Glenwood, Illinois, I wrote her every day and couldn't wait for her letters. She was assigned to childcare staff at Wycliffe's summer linguistic-translation courses at the University of Oklahoma at Norman. I drove from home to the campus in the 1950 Ford that I had previously purchased from my grandparents. I had bought an engagement ring, but decided not to take it with me lest I be tempted to move too quickly in our relationship. After a short time with her, however, I called my Mom and asked her to send the ring. During that trip to visit Margaret, I proposed, and we were engaged on July 5. With Margaret being from Oregon and me from Illinois, any travel for our families was complicated. With that in mind, we decided to get married at the English-speaking Union Church in Mexico City where Margaret attended and taught Sunday School.

Mt. Rainier, near Centralia, Washington, where Margaret spent her teen years

Married in Mexico

1958

We married in Mexico City on September 27, 1958. My parents, Eno and Dorothy Zander, graciously lent me their new 1958 Chevrolet to make the drive from Glenwood, Illinois. My brother, Billy, was best man. Two of the four single women from our evening meals at the translation center served as bridesmaids. Margaret, the bride, was beautiful in her lovely white dress. We exchanged our vows in English.

A few "friends," determined to prevent a smooth newlywed getaway, disabled the cars of the wedding party parked in front of the church. Anticipating these practical jokers, I had hidden our car off-site in a location known only to me and friend Bob Chaney. Our exit was being watched, but as the practical joker watching the back door went back for seconds on wedding cake, Margaret and I slipped out the back door, rendezvoused with Bob, and made a clean getaway. Friends saw Billy off for his return flight to Chicago.

We traveled around Mexico for our honeymoon, ending up in Acapulco the night a hurricane hit. When we got to town the rain was pouring down, and the wind was blowing hard. All the lights in the city were out. The city was shut down, restaurants and hotels were closed, and things looked bleak. We managed to find a hotel room, registered in candlelight, and retired without dinner. The weather improved, and we enjoyed the clear sunny day that followed.

Forrest and Margaret were married at Union Church of Mexico City, September 27, 1958.

Our trip in the new car continued via Texas, Arizona, and California, to Springbrook, Oregon, where I met Margaret's family: her mother, sister, two brothers, and their families. Wow! I had gained a whole new family. I attended her Quaker (Evangelical Friends) Church, and enjoyed the Pacific Northwest for the first time. Situated in the Willamette River Valley, with mountains, hills, and lush valleys, and with Mt. Hood and other snow caps in the distance, the view from her home was spectacular.

It was an unequaled experience for this Midwesterner who was accustomed to flat farmlands, where you can see for miles in any direction.

After three weeks in Oregon, we then traveled to Wyoming to meet former neighbors and friends from when the Morgan family farmed there. Then on to Rubio, Iowa, to meet most of the Morgan clan who populated many farms in the area known as Washington County.

Heading to the mission field

1958-1959

We settled temporarily in my hometown, Glenwood, Illinois, where we purchased and packed for four years on the field. My dad was the expert packer, getting more into our barrels and crates than we thought they could hold. I remember him with a barrel heaped several inches above the rim. He proceeded to put the top on the heap and with the hydraulic jack from his truck against a horizontal beam in the basement, made the overflow compress until the lid was sealed. We ended up with 18 barrels and 5 crates, including household items, baby stroller, high chair and clothes, an amateur radio transceiver and beam antenna, and my big tool box and roll-away full of aircraft maintenance tools. My home church in Glenwood had graced us with a gift shower, providing many items from a list they had previously requested. Dad hauled it all to a trucking terminal in Chicago, where it went to a seaport and ended up in Lima, Peru, some months later.

Airline tickets in hand, we drove a dealer's car to Miami. The dealer, learning that I was a pilot, offered me $2,500 to fly a load of arms to Cuba. (No, thanks!) We didn't know if it was for the dictator Bautista or for Fidel Castro. We didn't wait to find out.

On January 1, 1959, we attended the Orange Bowl Game between Oklahoma and Syracuse and enjoyed the halftime festivities celebrating 25 years. On January 2 we boarded an APA (Peruvian Airlines) DC-4, a four engine piston-powered airliner at the Miami International Airport. Our first scheduled stop was to be Havana, Cuba, but we overflew the capital due to the civil war. Fidel Castro was scheduled to arrive there that day. We later stopped for fuel and passengers in Panama City and Medellin, Colombia. After fourteen hours, we arrived late at night at Limatambo International Airport in Lima, Peru.

At long last we were together on our first mission field. We then discovered that there were several Wycliffe missionaries on the same flight but unknown to each other. We were greeted royally by our mission colleagues. The ladies received bouquets of beautiful roses, and we were whisked off to the Lima Guest House, ready for Spanish study.

Language study

1959

To be a pilot in South America, I needed to know Spanish. That's one reason we moved to Lima, Peru—to study Spanish for five months. The other reason was that Peru had a flight program with experienced jungle pilots and mechanics who would be my mentors during our first months on the field.

On our second day in Peru, we were taken to the home of the Vizcardo family, where we lived and learned for the next five months. The Vizcardos were a lovely family of Sergio and Maruja, with a 10-year-old daughter Eliana, a cook Julia, and a maid Jesus.

But we started out at close to zero in the language. I only knew a few words, and Margaret wasn't much further along than that. We were learning Spanish from scratch. Yet we were sitting around a table with a Spanish-speaking family and eating meals with them. We didn't even know the words for the food, much less what to say to them. We were in classes from 8:30 to 11:15 AM, and then we were expected to spend 6-8 more hours daily on homework, listening to tapes, memorizing dialogues, and conversing with those in the household.

Julia prepared all the meals. We were served breakfast by ourselves, and then dinner and supper with the family, providing good opportunities to hear and speak the language. We learned quickly with good instructors and interaction at meals. Dinner was always soup first, followed by the main course and fruit for dessert. Supper was two main courses consisting of some type of meat and lots of white rice. You would think we were in China! I quickly tired of the rice and could hardly face it another meal. Finally, I asked if there was any ketchup in the house. Boy, that sure helped with the rice, and the family thought I was so smart. Sergio tried it, liked it, pointed to his head, gestured to me, and said, "Forrest, muy inteligente."

The Vizcardos were good to us. Sergio found out we liked basketball, so he took us to see the Globetrotters play a local team. Fun! And one of the Globetrotters was a player I had watched play at Bloom Township High School, my alma mater.

We took the Vizcardos out for dinner at an American restaurant to celebrate their anniversary. They were like kids at a circus. This was a rare treat for them. To show their gratitude, they reciprocated by inviting a dozen or so relatives over for supper to meet us.

We also learned some difficult lessons while we were there, like not to go to the beach and stay for four hours. I was so sunburned that I became sick and ran a fever.

We were tasked with traveling around the city and learning all we could of the culture and language. Our travel was by streetcar or taxi. One day, while we were on a streetcar, a gang of six men boarded and waited for us to disembark. They let Margaret off and then crowded me into a corner and went for my pockets. Realizing they were pickpockets, I reached my hand for my wallet and grabbed a hand! I started yelling for the police. I saved the billfold and thought we were home free. Later, I found that they had stolen my credential case with licenses and important papers (pilot, mechanic, drivers, radio licenses; draft and social security cards—12 important documents altogether). We were thankful it wasn't any worse and lost only 100 soles ($4) that was with the credentials. Even so, it was a daunting task to replace all those documents, but I had no choice. We advertised for it in the newspapers and on the radio, but to no avail. After that, I never carried a wallet. Instead I carried a little money and walked around with my hand in my pocket.

His Faithfulness Reaches to the Skies

About this time, Margaret wrote home: "Every week it seems, we hear reports of the enemy's work through various individuals and antagonistic groups to thwart the Lord's work here and get us out of the country. Only the Lord is keeping His work going and preserving our group here. The enemy is determined to prevent the Indians from hearing and having God's Word in their languages but we're so thankful that God is on our side and gives victory and advances His work after every attack."

To facilitate getting to daily classes in the center of Lima, we bought a motor scooter. This eliminated the long walk to the bus or streetcar stop. We were out practicing riding our new vehicle when a neighbor's huge dog came for us from behind at full speed with big teeth and a fierce bark. Unaccustomed to the foot gearshift, I could not get it into a lower gear to speed away. The dog closed in with Margaret's leg the closest body part to bite. The dog was right behind us, and I still could not shift gears. Finally, in desperation, I jammed on the brake. The dog plowed head on into the rear of the scooter, got a huge bump on the head, and slunk away in defeat. Whew!

One day, we were walking down the street in Lima wearing identical shirts, gifts from my sister at Christmas. Talk about attracting attention! This was so unusual that people hung out of the taxis and streetcars staring at us as they went by.

As our time in Lima began to draw to a close, we shared our faith with Sergio and Maruja since we had become more fluent in the language and could point them to appropriate Scriptures in Spanish New Testaments. They attended an evangelistic service with us, and we prayed for their salvation.

Before leaving Lima for the jungle, I went through the process of complying with all the rules to get my pilot license. Although they recognized my U.S. Commercial Pilot License, I still needed to go through the hoops to qualify in Peru.

The psychological test was especially interesting. Question 1: What would you want to be if you were not a human being? My answer: a lion. Why? So I could be the king of the beasts. Question 2: What would you not want to be? A mosquito. Why? One swat and it would be all over. Question 3: If you had to die, how would you like it to happen? Question 4: How would you not like to die?

I guess I was considered sane and got the license.

Chapter 2

LIFE AS A MISSIONARY PILOT

Stranded!

1959

I could hardly believe it.

We were stuck in a rut on a jungle road. When I got out to take a look at our predicament, I found myself at the bottom of the deepest rut I had ever seen in a road—five feet deep. The road's surface was even with my shoulders.

Trucks supplying the jungle towns from the capital city of Lima, Peru, used this section of unpaved highway to cross the Andes Mountains on a daily basis. But during the rainy season, it became almost impassable in a cargo truck, much less in a standard vehicle like the one we were driving.

How did we ever get into this? Five of us Wycliffe missionaries were passengers in a new carryall van given to our mission by a church in Michigan. Paul and Esther Powlison, Wycliffe missionaries supported by the church, were driving it to Yarinacocha, the jungle mission center. Invited by the Powlisons, my wife, Margaret, and I looked forward to our new work in the jungle after this trip. We were joined by a single missionary,

Dean Sawdon.

But now the van was hopelessly stuck in the mud. We thought we would avoid getting stuck by straddling some of the deep ruts. That worked for a while, but now the van refused to move. Night was falling, the closest refuge nowhere to be seen. Where would we sleep? In the van of course! Dean slept in the front seat with part of his body under the steering wheel. Paul and Esther, veteran missionaries and translators to a jungle Indian tribe, did the courteous thing. They put us in the wider rear seat, and they took the middle seat only 2/3s as wide. But neither seat was built to sleep two. As night fell, we settled into our cramped spaces as best we could.

Sleep escaped us as we tried to adjust in our narrow quarters. Well into the night, we heard raucous snoring. Margaret poked me. "It's not me," I said. Esther's poke in the next seat generated Paul's remark, "It's not me." Obviously, Dean was fast asleep and enjoying it.

Dawn came as welcome relief. Dragging our tired bodies out of the van, we looked underneath. The spare tire had vibrated loose and became like the blade of a bulldozer. We were dragging a load of mud. No wonder the van was stuck! Once we solved that problem, the van began moving and we climbed aboard, only to get stuck again.

Paul and Esther, knowing the highway, remembered a missionary couple with a ministry to local people. They lived somewhere on the road ahead. We abandoned the van and began walking. After some miles, we found Louie and Rhoda Rankin's house. They graciously welcomed five new guests, and there we stayed while the rains abated and the highway dried out.

The normal trip from Lima was about three days. But we were into the trip some eight days and unable to communicate our whereabouts. As far as the director and missionaries at the Center were concerned, we could have driven over a steep precipice or been taken hostage by bandits.

How would we let them know we were okay? This was long before cell phones, satellite phones, or the Internet. There was no way to text, instant message, email, or otherwise get a message out to the people who were concerned about our delay.

What we did have was shortwave. Louie showed me his transceiver. Unfortunately, it wasn't working. Having learned some electronics basics at Moody Bible Institute as part of the Missionary Aviation Course, I knew some radio theory. I had learned enough to get my ham radio license, and I built my first transmitter in Moody's lab. Maybe my rustic knowledge would come in handy. I searched the shortwave band for Yarinacocha's aircraft frequency on which they followed the planes flying over the jungle. I tuned in the operator's voice confirming position reports from the mission aircraft. If only I could talk to them. But when I tuned up the transmitter, I found that Louie was right. The voice (audio) portion of the transmitter had failed.

Then the Lord planted an idea in my mind. Using the microphone button for a telegraph key, I started sending Morse code. It took a few seconds for the operator to recognize code on the voice frequency. Then he answered, "Who is calling?" Proficient in code, he received the information that we were safe and staying at the Rankin place. We would attempt to drive the van in a few days when the road dried out. The three-day trip took eleven days.

We arrived safely at Yarinacocha Center to begin our new ministry with Wycliffe. I learned that the Lord builds into our lives all kinds of know-how and experience. Some are immediately useful, and some lie in the mental storage room. We were sure glad the radio operator knew Morse code, and that I hadn't slept through code class at Moody.

"Hazel" and the corn flakes

1960-1962

From Peru, we were reassigned to Ecuador. In March, 1960, we moved to the jungle mission center, Limoncocha, Ecuador, where I served as a missionary pilot, while Margaret taught missionary children and served as Center hostess. Since I was busy flying and Margaret was busy teaching, we hired a woman to prepare meals. (She later cared for our baby and any missionary kids who happened to be staying with us.) This woman was trained by Elisabeth Elliot, widow of missionary martyr Jim Elliot. We called our employee "Hazel" because she was just like the "Hazel" on television. She would tell us what to do, when to do it, and how to do it.

One time we had a house guest who wanted to show appreciation by buying us a special gift. So she bought us a box of cornflakes. In those days, cornflakes were very expensive in Ecuador. One could hardly afford to buy them. What a rare

His Faithfulness Reaches to the Skies

treat!

Margaret said to Hazel, "We have a box of cornflakes here that we will have for breakfast." When Hazel came out of the kitchen, we looked at her tray of steaming bowls and knew something was wrong. Sure enough, Hazel had prepared the corn flakes just like she made oatmeal, by pouring them in a pot of water and boiling them.

Maria, Secoya woman in Ecuador, dressing Margaret in native costume including face paint

Cargo

1960-1962

A huge cargo plane arrived in Shell Mera, Ecuador, with a load of bull calves. Now it was our job to fly them out to surrounding jungle mission stations. The first calf must have been borne by an elephant. A missionary asked us to fly it to his village.

No ordinary calf, this one weighed 600 pounds! Almost a full load in our small mission plane. Not only that, but we were accustomed to flying nonliving cargo. There's a big difference between 600 pounds of dead weight and a living, moving animal. What if we got to 4,000 feet and the bull decided flying wasn't fun? Seat belts restrained human passengers. But not a 600-pound animal. We needed help.

But the missionary did, too. The Shuar Indians, former head-hunters, needed domesticated meat to replace the jungle animals, which by that time were in short supply. As the jungle population increased, hunting and fishing no longer sustained the Shuar people.

Descended from Brahma (Cebu) cattle brought from India, the male calf was already accustomed to hot, humid climates. Revitalizing bloodlines of local cattle, his offspring would supply both milk and meat. Selling cattle would add to the local economy.

We really wanted to help the missionary. But how?

A veterinarian volunteered to tie the calf's four feet together with a heavy rope. He also injected it with a strong tranquilizer. We fastened the monster down to the frame of the airplane with a big nylon retaining net, snapped into place where the rear seat normally fastened. Now our cargo could barely move. As first-term freshman missionary pilot, I would fly the plane while our chief pilot sat in the copilot's seat with a loaded pistol, just in case.

With the calf safely secured, we took off and began our climb to cruising altitude. Apparently, however, the tranquilizer hadn't completely taken effect. To our surprise, the 600 pound monster began to move under the retaining net. We could feel the whole airplane move from side to side as our lively load shifted his weigh under the net.

Now what? Return and land with a shifting cargo? Not a realistic option! We decided to continue toward the missionary's airstrip in the jungle, hoping for the best. As the tranquilizer began to have its full effect, the calf relaxed and soon fell fast asleep.

We made an easy landing and began to unload. The sleeping animal refused to awaken and now became dead weight. We wrestled it out of the plane and untied its legs. There it lay—a different kind of sleeping beauty!

After some jostling and cajoling, our sleeping giant rose slowly and staggered off, led on a rope by our happy missionary and his Shuar friends. Soon our unusual passenger's offspring would revolutionize the jungle cattle industry in that area and provide a better way of life for an impoverished jungle people.

Mission accomplished!

Flying that animal contributed to the missionary's ministry. Along with preaching, he demonstrated his love for the Shuar people by practical acts of kindness, by meeting needs beyond their capacity to handle. In doing so, he developed deep, abiding relationships with the people. Sometimes, the things we do for others in the name of Christ can speak louder than our words. Together, our kind acts of service build relationships and give credibility to our verbal witness.

We flew other strange cargo: pigs, Peppie the parrot, baby chicks, dogs, you name it. If it fit through the door, we flew it.

One time we flew a bulldozer. I didn't see how it would be possible. But, after removing the big heavy tracks and the engine, we reduced each piece to a one-flight load. After several flights with the "pieces," the missionary reassembled the bulldozer at his mission station. He used it to eventually extend the airstrip so larger planes could land. Good for him!

Later he wanted us to fly a huge transmitter out to his jungle village. It was humongous! I thought, *You don't expect us to fly that in our plane*. We tried to put it in the plane, but it wouldn't fit. It stuck out by a foot. The door wouldn't close.

I was ready to tell him, "No!" But I was just a freshman missionary pilot. Fortunately, our chief pilot, Don Smith, was there. He had lots of experience. He had a solution.

Take off the door? Smitty, you've got to be kidding, I thought.

"Yes," Smitty said. "You can fly an airplane without the door. We'll also remove the metal front and back panels so just the angle iron is sticking out." He explained that the air could pass through the opening and cause minimal drag.

Smitty continued, "We'll take off and, after we break ground, we'll fly low over the airstrip and check to see that none of the critical control characteristics are altered. If we sense a problem, we're only a foot off the airstrip and can land. If not, we'll climb out and deliver the goods."

It worked out just as he said it would. As a result, the former headhunters of the Ecuadorian jungles, the Shuar people, would hear the gospel in their own language. Tiny transistor radios, pre-tuned to the missionary's frequency, were distributed to many Shuar Indians along those jungle rivers. Lives changed. Believers were discipled, and weeks of travel eliminated!

Strange cargo? Yes, but, wow, I'm glad we made that flight!

Fuel

One day I landed, refueled, loaded, and taxied to the active runway for takeoff. After the normal preflight check and engine run-up, I took off. Everything seemed normal until I looked at the fuel gauges. At takeoff, the wing tanks had been full. Now, a few minutes later, they were indicating half full. I quickly returned and landed. When I got out to look around, the problem was obvious. The wing tank caps were not secured and hung by their chain retainers away from the wing tanks. The reduced pressure on top of the wing allowed the fuel to be sucked out at a high rate. If I had flown just a few minutes farther, I would have been forced to crash land in the jungle. Even though the employee who had serviced the aircraft while I loaded the cargo had failed to secure the gas caps, it was my responsibility as pilot-in-command to check them during my preflight walk-around inspection.

I made a mistake that could have been fatal. But the Lord was gracious, and brought the problem to my attention before it was too late.

Very scared passenger

We operated from some short airstrips in Ecuador. One was at Dureno among the Cofan people. Translators Bub and Bobbie Borman were in the early stages of learning the Cofan language and needed to be in the village. But they were unable to be there for a time, so they arranged for a lady from the village to travel to their location so they could have continued exposure to the language. I was asked to fly to Dureno, pick her up, and transport her to their location.

I landed safely on the tiny Dureno airstrip about 600 feet long. There was the lady, ready to travel, dressed in typical Cofan dress. I noticed her long skirt and blouse, the flowers on her wrists and ankles, her painted face, long tropical bird feathers in her perforated ears, and another long bird feather in her nose. She wore several necklaces made of beautiful jungle materials like iridescent beetle wings and seed pods from a particular tree.

I put her in the co-pilot seat beside me and taxied to the end of the short runway. I went through my takeoff checklist: Twenty degrees of flaps, auxiliary fuel pump on, engine controls at maximum rpm. Time for takeoff. I looked down this reduced piece of real estate. At the other end there was a drop-off, followed by large boulders, a rocky beach, and then a river and tall trees. I had a few critical seconds on takeoff to make all the right decisions. If I messed up the takeoff, it would ruin the whole flight!

His Faithfulness Reaches to the Skies

Focusing on a safe departure, I held the brakes, pushed the throttle forward, and checked the engine instruments for full power: 3,400 rpm and 28 inches of manifold pressure. All OK.

Releasing the brakes, I started down the bumpy jungle runway. Halfway down, the woman became so frightened that she reached over and grabbed my arm. Suddenly I was in a wrestling match at the most critical point of the takeoff. I quickly ripped my arm out of her grasp and got my hand back on the flight controls.

I eased back on the controls as we reached the end. Clearing the drop-off, rocks, river, and tall trees, I started my climb for altitude. That's the point at which, in a commercial flight, the pilot checks on the comfort of his passengers. I looked over at my frightened passenger and…oh, my! She had pulled her skirt up over her head.

Now what do I do? My instructors at Moody tried to prepare us for any eventuality in missionary flying. But they hadn't prepared me for this situation.

I kept my eyes on the instruments on my side of the cockpit, and avoided looking at my passenger. After a time I became concerned for her. No doubt this was her first time in an airplane. Realizing how scared she must be, I glanced over to check on her.

To my great relief, she had worn two skirts![2]

---

[2] Sometime later I mentioned this incident to the Bormans. They assured me it was customary for Cofan women to wear two skirts.

Left: Cofan woman similar to the one so scared on takeoff that she grabbed my arm and then put her skirt over her head.
Right: Bub and Bobbie Borman family

Margaret with her first grade class, Omar Johnson, Larry Allen, and Randy Borman, in their jungle school house with bark floors and walls and palm leaf roof.

Unexpected ministry opportunities

1960-1962

Along with our other duties in flying and hosting guests, Margaret and I served as houseparents for David, Mary, and Jonathan Lindskoog for an entire school year. Their parents, John and Carrie, were learning the Cayapa language far away on the western coast of Ecuador. We agreed to take care of the children who were attending the missionary kids' school at the Limoncocha Center. With no school-age children of our own, learning parenting skills proved interesting. But we took on the challenge of fixing meals, helping with homework, establishing boundaries and expectations, and sharing fun activities.

I decided to start an AWANA program for David and Jonathan. We added to the group other boys who were kids of the other pilots and missionaries living on the center. I appealed to my boyhood friend, Joe DeWaard, who was leader of the AWANA program at my home church in Glenwood, Illinois. Joe was a wonderful friend and helped out by providing the materials, awards, and uniforms for our boys. At our weekly meetings, we played the same games, memorized the same Scriptures, and tried to guide our boys in the same activities as their counterparts in Glenwood.

Juan Guevara and his family also lived at Limoncocha. Juan was employed at our hangar as a mechanic-in-training and all around helper. He assisted in refueling the aircraft, learned basic mechanic skills, and gave us additional practice with our Spanish as we conversed on a daily basis. There was no Spanish-speaking church in the area, so I decided to have a weekly

Bible study with Juan in our home. We enjoyed studying the Scriptures together. Years later, Juan moved to a remote community in the mountains and became pastor to a church there. I like to think that our Bible study contributed to his pastoral ministry. Likewise, all of us never know how our investment of time and resources for the Kingdom will bear fruit years, decades, even generations later.

Expecting our first child, Forrest Jr.

1960

We were excited when we received the news that Margaret was pregnant. What would it be like to hold that new baby, to look into his eyes, and to see the beauty of God's tiny creation? It was a wonderful time of anticipation. My parents were elated, too—their first grandchild was on the way. My mom and sister, Beverly, bought airline tickets and planned to arrive in Quito soon after the baby was born.

Even Hazel was excited. She came up with a name for him before he was born. Since Wawa is the Quichua word for baby, Hazel, assuming the child would be a boy, coined the word, "Fori-wa," meaning "Baby Forrey."

A tragic loss

1960-1961

Our first child, Forrest Jr., was born at the HCJB Hospital in Quito. When our son was about nine weeks old, we traveled to

His Faithfulness Reaches to the Skies

Limoncocha, the mission's center of operations. The baby was fussy. It looked like he was coming down with something. We thought it might be the flu. Of course, we checked it out with the nurse.

The nurse was sure he had the flu.

"The Indians in the village have had the flu," she told us. "He's probably caught it. Don't worry. It's your first baby. You're probably overly concerned."

But, after three days, Forrest Jr. didn't improve, so we flew him an hour away to the HCJB Jungle Hospital in Shell Mera. When we arrived, the doctor examined him and said, "He doesn't have the flu. He has a strangulated hernia."

He needed emergency surgery. But we had waited three days. Was it too late?

We sat out in the hall and prayed while his surgery was going on, hoping for the best. After the surgery, through the night, and on into the next day, we waited and prayed. But the three-day delay before surgery proved fatal. The doctor came out and said, "We did everything we could, but your little boy has died."

I asked to see my son.

I still remember holding him for the last time. Gently kissing his forehead, I bid our beautiful baby boy goodbye for the last time on earth. I can still see our missionary pilot friends, digging the grave out back in the middle of pouring rain.

This may have been the most difficult experience of our lives. To lose our first child and to think, maybe we could have done more—if only we had known.

In the middle of this second-guessing, one of the HCJB missionaries, came to see me, and gave me a word from the Lord —a word that helped me through those days of loss and grief.

"Forrest," he said, "you don't understand why this happened at this point, but someday you'll be able to say that you wouldn't have wanted it to be any other way."

I can't honestly say that I've arrived at that point yet, but I know that someday, even if it's with the Lord, I will be able to say that.

Margaret took the baby's death with great bravery, yet with deep sadness and grief. Even years later, when his birthday came around, she would weep. When home on furlough we would include a brief mention of his death and his photo in our slide presentation of our life and experiences on the field. Each time, she would be moved to tears.

Forrest Jr. was buried in Shell Mera, Ecuador, next to the grave of a Waorani Indian, a relative of one of the men who massacred Nate Saint and four other missionaries in 1956.

After the funeral and burial in Shell Mera, we took a few days off and flew to Quito. We needed time to grieve and adjust to his untimely death. It would have been easy to go on home to the USA. Our family, friends, and churches would have understood the trauma we had experienced in losing our first beloved son. But God had called us to Ecuador and even this tragedy would not deter us from staying with our calling. We were assured via ham radio that many were praying, and the prayers of God's people helped to keep us focused on the task and calling.

God never makes a mistake

1961

An encouraging incident happened as we were waiting in Shell Mera for our flight to Quito. We met Enrique, an airline employee, assisting passengers. I told him in Spanish about the baby's death and our hope of seeing him someday in heaven. As I shared the Gospel story with Enrique, his heart was open and he received Christ right there at the airport. Remembering the value that the Lord showed for one lost soul, I then told him that if our baby's death had contributed to his newfound faith, it would have been worth this tremendous loss.

This statement made a deep impression on Enrique. Later he showed up at the Limoncocha center and became an employee of our mission for a time. As he shared his testimony in a prayer meeting, it was translated into English for some of our missionaries who weren't fluent in Spanish. When Enrique came to the part about the baby's death contributing to his salvation, the missionary wept as he translated. I understood it in both languages, and for me, it has been a wonderful confirmation that God never makes a mistake. He can take the worst tragedy and bring hope and light to the lost and to those He loves.

Forrest Zander

Cofan Indian men (Ecuador)

Names

1960-1962

People all over the world are fascinated by names. This was true of people in the language groups in South America. I was humbled and honored when a Cofan couple in Ecuador named their first child after me. They asked the translators my name, actually my nickname, which in English is Forrey, short for Forrest. They spelled it "Fori" following Spanish phonetics. In Cofan, however, the pronunciation pattern did not allow them to say my name without injecting a glottal stop and another vowel between the "Fo" and "ri" so it came out as Fo?ari, making it sound like three syllables.

An interesting custom among the Cofan people is that when the first baby is born to a family, the parents take on the new-born's name. So the mother of this baby became FoʔariQuitsa (Forrey's mother) and the father's name became Foʔari Chan. I'm honored to have three Cofan people carrying my name.

Anna Marie's birth

1961

Later in 1961, we were expecting our second child. November 25, 1961, dawned bright and clear in Ecuador with me, the expectant father, in the jungles. The mother-in-waiting was 100 miles away, close to the hospital in Quito. But I figured we were safe because the due date was still some three weeks away.

It had been a week of heavy flying for me, including flying guests to the first baptismal service in the Auca-Waorani village of Tiwaeno. By Saturday I felt the need for a change. I joined two other companions for a day of hunting in the deep jungle. But "just in case," we took a radio receiver and gave one of the other pilots instructions to fly overhead to tell us about any change in the baby's scheduled arrival.

We were several hours upriver at about 2 PM when we heard the drone of a low flying airplane. The pilot radioed the news. Margaret was in the hospital. The baby could arrive before midnight.

Panic set in.

The driver put the outboard motor, attached to a dugout canoe, into high gear as we literally flew back down the river. The trip that took four hours one way took less than half that time the other way. A friend with a motor scooter, waiting at the canoe landing, whisked me home to pack. The airplane, waiting to carry me to Quito, would make a valiant effort to beat the stork and the airport closing time of 6 PM.

Meanwhile, things were getting tense at the hospital. Mother-to-be was experiencing complications, and the doctor, out of town on a one-day trip, encountered car trouble on the way home. Let's just say that Margaret was a little perturbed at me for leaving my post of waiting; she was sure she would have the baby alone.

As Margaret lay there, the clouds settled lower and lower over the mountains surrounding the hospital. Airport rules prohibited flying after 6 PM in that mountainous area. My plane had left Limoncocha at the last possible minute to make the 6 PM landing deadline in Quito. As we climbed over the jungles toward the Andes Mountains, cloud coverage became a major concern. A mountain pass between an 18,000-foot snow-capped peak (El Cayambe) on one side, and a 17,000-foot peak (Antisana) on the other, seemed full of clouds. The shrinking minutes on the clock left no time to deviate and find an alternate entrance. As we approached that mountain pass with our Helio Courier airplane, at the last minute we saw a passageway between cloud layers at about 13,000 feet. Using that, we slipped into the Quito valley. The aircraft touched down at precisely 6 PM in light rain. I hailed the first taxi I could find and arrived at the hospital "on time."

At 6:30 PM Margaret heard someone running down the hall. I arrived just as the nurses rolled her into the delivery room. By this time, the primary physician had also arrived. I shaved while hospital staff made preparations for a "C" section, due to a possible "placenta-first" complication. But Anna Marie (Anita) Zander popped out of her own accord at 7:30 PM. Eleven months after our first baby died, Anna Marie was born. We call her "Anita," Spanish for "lovable little Anna."

Tree frog

1961

Like any other parents, we lost our share of sleep when our babies were nursing or fussy due to illness. Margaret took the brunt of this as I fled to the guest room so I could fly safely the next day. But the greatest hindrance to sleep was a tree frog. It began its shrill call at bedtime and continued every ten to fifteen minutes all night until daybreak. The creature set up shop in the jungle right outside our house, but I could not locate it. When I tried throwing something in its direction, the noise stopped it for a short time. Then it was back. I resorted to the shotgun, firing it in the direction of the noise. This helped a little more, but it would begin again after a bit longer time. Night after night this went on. Finally, I stayed up and located the tree from which the noise originated. Then I waited

Jungle bird called Macaw (Guacamayo in Spanish)

until it started calling again. I spotted its eyes with a flashlight and fired the shotgun. Silence reined for the entire night. What a relief!

Army ants

1960-1962

In Ecuador we lived for three years in a thatch-roofed house. The roof was made with palm leaves. The floors and walls were made of bark. Our baby, Anita, learned to walk on a bouncy bark floor.

Though our home was up on posts, that didn't keep out army ants. When the army ants came, we evacuated our house and let the ants march on through. There was nothing anyone could do to stop the determined insects. When a column of ants showed up, we grabbed the baby, ran outside, and waited for them to pass.

Having army ants wasn't all bad though, because they cleaned out the house as they went. That meant they took the cockroaches with them.

Having fun

1960-62

What do you do in your spare time when you are in the jungle, far from all the amenities of civilization? There were plenty of things we could NOT do: watch sports on TV, go to the mall, bowl, or golf. We could NOT visit with our families, as they lived thousands of miles away. One limiting factor was daylight: In the tropics night begins almost immediately at sunset. There was hardly any twilight. Our center generator gave us lights until about 9 PM. Then it was bedtime until sunup at 6 AM. The evenings were spent writing letters to family, playing board games, or enjoying amateur radio.

Otherwise, some of my favorite leisure activities included hunting, fishing, gardening, and Scrabble.

Gator hunting

1960-62

Another favorite activity was alligator (cayman) hunting. Our lake at Limoncocha, Ecuador, was full of them.[3] We approached our prey in a dugout canoe with a rifle and flashlights. There were areas along the lakeshore where floating vegetation made an ideal habitat for alligators. Silently and slowly we approached and shined our flashlights right where the vegetation ended and open water began. Two bright orange eyes reflected the light and gave away the hiding creature. Flashlight off, we would head for that location in the darkness, rifle in hand, as a companion slowly paddled our canoe closer. Flashlight on, and the creature would usually be transfixed by the beam. As long as the beam wasn't broken by some movement, it would allow our approach.

Our target was between those eyes. Shoot, and then quickly grab the dead or wounded alligator before it sank, and toss it

---
3In those days there were no hunting restrictions, and the idea of endangered species wasn't on anybody's radar.

into the canoe. The next moment could be very risky if the alligator was merely stunned. We needed to grab it behind the head and hit it hard with a club. The three to five foot ones were best both for the tail meat, almost like lobster, and for the belly skin that made great leather products. I sent several skins to the tanner in Quito where they were made into a pair of dress shoes and matching purse for Margaret.

One time as I shot the creature and grabbed for it before it sank, my hand went right into its mouth. Fortunately, it was small and its teeth produced only scratches as I withdrew my hand and threw the animal into the canoe.

Occasionally we spotted a set of eyes six or eight inches apart —a huge and dangerous animal. A guest once shot one that was thirteen feet long. A shotgun was the indicated weapon. These large gators did not often expose themselves. To get them to emerge from hiding, we would look for a baby gator maybe a foot long. When we held it by the tail, it would make a squeaky distress sound. Silently paddling near the floating vegetation, we would look for the big eyes. They would come out to "rescue" the baby in distress. A big, long monster once came out and surfaced in open water on the lake side of the canoe. A guest shot it, and it sank. Deciding not to pursue it in the dark, the guest returned the next day and was able to bring it to the surface with a long pole and big hook. It measured over eleven feet.

Fishing

1960-62

Margaret and I also enjoyed fishing in the lake. She had the record for the largest corbina, a bass-like tropical fresh-water variety, weighing about 4 pounds. The piranha (*caribe* in Spanish) were the most dangerous. I remember catching my first piranha about 8-9 inches long. I cut off the head and opened its mouth to admire its beautiful set of teeth. Big mistake! The head reflexed and its powerful jaw bit my finger down to the bone. I still have the scar to prove it.

Forrest, Margaret, and Anita, at jungle center, Limoncocha, Ecuador

Forrest Zander

Communication via ham radio

1960s and 1970s

We were on the mission field long before the Internet, email, Skype, Facebook, Twitter, instant messaging, cell phones, satellite phones, or any of the many technologies that make it easy to stay in touch with people all over the world. But I did have a ham radio license, and enjoyed looking for other ham radio operators around the world, especially those who lived close to our parents and other extended family members. Sometimes I would find a ham with a phone patch. We could talk into the microphone in Colombia, and our family would hear us in Illinois. It was one-way. When ready to listen, we would say "over" and hear that person's voice coming back to us. The grandparents were especially grateful to hear the voices of their beloved grandchildren as well as our voices. It was a great encouragement to us to get news from home and maintain this kind of contact. There was one ham in my hometown of Glenwood, Illinois, who would stand by for us on Saturday afternoons at a specific time and frequency. He was a special blessing to us in the foreign country and to family at home.

Another aspect of ham radio that I really enjoyed was talking to operators in rare and distant countries. Before leaving for South America I had earned an award for working all the U.S. states, all continents, and had contacted a total of 102 countries from my home call, W9FTL. There was a recognition certificate for working 100 countries called the DX Century Club (DXCC) Award. Unfortunately, I only received QSL (confirmation) cards from 98 countries. Operating from the jungles of Ecuador, I had a very rare and sought-after call, HC7FZ, which

67

was desired by hams in the U.S. and other countries, working for the DXCC and other certificates. Whenever I was on the air, there were pileups of stations trying to reach me. It was fun being a "rare commodity."

Baby Anita's first birthday party: You can probably pick Anita out of the crowd.

Anita's first birthday

1962

Margaret and Hazel were busy planning Anita's first-birthday party. Hazel was instructed to invite a "few" Quichua friends from the nearby village. Seems the whole village came—146 people! The total guest list included speakers of five languages from three tribes. But Margaret and Hazel rose to the occasion. Snacks included 20 dozen cookies, five gallons of lemonade, seven loaves of bread, six cans of tuna and four bags of candy. We played games and ate snacks, and everybody had a great time.

His Faithfulness Reaches to the Skies

Chapter 3

AMAZING TRANSFORMATION

Former murderers become friends

Prior to 1960

On January 11, 1956, the *New York Times* ran the headline, "Five U.S. Missionaries Lost; Jungle Murder Feared." The events surrounding this story have become part of church history, and they became closely intertwined with our lives.

During the 1940s in the jungles of Ecuador, oil companies were prospecting for petroleum. They wanted to enter the territory of a people group known to outsiders as the Auca ("savage" in the language of a nearby people group, the Quichua). The Auca did not want outsiders in their territory. So they devised a method to keep foreigners out. Anyone who crossed their borders would be speared with hardwood spears.

Missionary pilot Nate Saint had his base of operations in Shell Mera, Ecuador (named after one of the oil companies), where his family lived with him. Nate was flying out to the jungle areas to serve the missionaries from several different missions. As he flew over Auca territory, about twenty minutes flying time from Shell Mera, he noticed houses out in the jungle and assumed they belonged to the Auca. The Lord gave him a burden to reach these people with the gospel of Christ. So he began to develop tactics for doing that.

His first plan involved a bucket drop. He lowered a bucket on a nylon cord from his circling airplane. He discovered an aerodynamic principle by which the bucket would go to the center of the circle. Then he would lower his altitude and he could actually drop the bucket on a specific spot in the jungle. Through the bucket drop, he was able to give the Auca people axe heads, machetes, and other gifts. Over time, the Aucas reciprocated and placed gifts in his bucket: things like feather jewelry, a baby parrot in a basket, and combs made from jungle materials.

Because the exchange of gifts was going so well, Nate felt that he had established a foundation for a friendly contact with these people. This was a secret mission. Most people did not know about it. He recruited four other missionaries to work with him: Pete Fleming, Jim Elliot, Roger Youdarian, and Ed McCully.

During his flights, Nate had discovered a beach exposed during the dry season on the Curaray River near an Auca village. Because he was such a skillful pilot, he was able to land his airplane on that tiny beach, which he named Palm Beach. He then shuttled his missionary partners there with materials, so they could build a tree house which would keep them dry in wet weather. In addition, if the Aucas turned belligerent, they would have a place to flee and protect themselves.

While the men were camped out on this beach, two Auca people appeared. The missionaries did not know their real names so they called them George and Delilah. George consented to

His Faithfulness Reaches to the Skies

an airplane ride, and Nate was able to fly him over his village. Unfortunately, the missionaries only knew a few phrases of the Auca language, so they couldn't actually communicate with them. After a while, these people disappeared into the jungle.

The missionaries hoped for a friendly contact with the Auca, but something tragic happened. Six Auca warriors returned to the beach with their hardwood spears, and all five of the missionaries were martyred. Although the missionaries had guns which they fired into the air to attempt to scare off the Auca people, they did not defend themselves with the bullets. They actually gave their lives so that these people who did not know Christ would have an opportunity for eternity with Him.

News of this event went out from HCJB radio to the whole world on shortwave. Our class of aviation students at Moody Bible Institute listened intently to the shortwave radio news broadcasts, first announcing the missionaries as missing, and then dead. Little did I know at the time that soon my life would intersect with the players in this historical event.

As the word went out, people became concerned for the Auca people, and believers began to pray. They prayed for the Auca people by name. In addition to prayer, at missions conferences across the USA, representatives of the families of the lost missionaries presented the need for others to take their places. Over the years I have met many missionaries from many mission boards who gave their lives to missions to take the place of these men in Ecuador. There was a great in-gathering of missionary men and women. This may have been the first indication that God was going to turn this tragedy into a triumph.

Meanwhile, two years before the missionaries were killed, Wycliffe translator Rachel Saint, the sister of the pilot, discovered an Auca woman named Dayuma at a ranch outside Auca territory. Dayuma had fled from her own people in fear of her life. Rachel began to live at the ranch and started learning the Auca language from this woman. Dayuma eventually became a Christian, the first Auca believer. However, when she was asked about building a bridge to her own tribe, she said, "I'll never go back to my people, because they'll spear me just like they did the missionaries."

But God worked in her heart, and after a while she said, "I will go at the risk of my life and try to make contact with my people." She went back to the village. It was about a two-day walk from the nearest airstrip called Arajuno. She went into the village of Tiwaino and was received in a friendly manner. She told them about this light-skinned woman who had learned their language and would like to live with them as well. When they gave permission, Dayuma went out to Arajuno and made contact. As a result, Rachel Saint, as well as Elizabeth Elliot (widow of Jim Elliot) and her little daughter, Valerie, began to live in the Tiwaino village with the Auca.

Rachel and Elizabeth became more fluent in the language, did some preliminary translation work, and taught the people the gospel. One by one, the Auca people began to believe. As a result of their work and Dayuma's, the five living killers of the missionaries on Palm Beach became believers.

Rachel and Elizabeth also learned that the term "Auca" is a derogatory word meaning "savage" in the Quichua language.

His Faithfulness Reaches to the Skies

The Auca people refer to themselves as the "Waorani" (sometimes spelled "Huaorani"), meaning "The People."

An airstrip for the Waorani (Auca)

1960

In March, 1960, four years after the missionaries were martyred, Margaret and I began our time of service in Ecuador. As a new missionary bush pilot, I was assigned to fly Bible translators to remote outposts in the same Amazonian jungles. Since Rachel Saint and Elizabeth Elliot had taken up residence in Tiwaeno, a Waorani (Auca) village that could only be reached by walking over a slippery rugged jungle trail for two exhausting days, they needed to build an airstrip. (The village got its name from the nearby Tiwaeno River.)

My first glimpse of the village was from the back of the airplane, rear door removed, and with a rope around my waist to keep me from falling into space through the large opening. I was surrounded by parts of a disassembled wheelbarrow, as Roy Gleason, the senior pilot at the controls, made low passes over a clearing near the village. Upon his hand signal, I threw the parts out the opening, hoping they would fall into the open field and could be retrieved by the people, who would then reassemble the wheelbarrow. During several passes we dropped axes, shovels, rakes, and machetes—everything the people would need to change that clearing into an airstrip.

About two months later, I was on final approach for landing at this new jungle airfield just over 600 feet long. (Our chief pilot made the real first landing, but this was my first landing.) It looks like a postage stamp as you're approaching it, but it gets a little bigger as you come closer. Once on the ground, I quickly snapped a photo to commemorate this historic moment in my life and career.

Huge jungle tree, 10 feet in diameter at its base, fell across a nearly completed airstrip. Removal required two more months of hard work.

Then the Waorani (Auca) people arrived en masse from the nearby village, some probably seeing a light-skinned man and a metallic "wood-bee" for the first time. Now normally the Waorani did not have much in the way of clothes, but when they heard the airplane was coming, they dressed up with mostly used clothes that people had given to Rachel. They found it very practical to have clothes in the jungle, because it keeps the mosquitoes away and keeps you warm, especially at night. The

Waorani had a real fascination for the airplane. In their language, they called it the "flying canoe," the "wood-bee," or the "metallic bee."

Quick thinking

1960-1962

One day while transporting Rachel, Chief Pilot Don Smith and I landed at the Arajuno airstrip serving the Quichua Indians. Because it was a long airstrip and just ten minutes away from the Waorani, it served as a gathering point if we were shuttling passengers or cargo. After shutting down the engine while still hot, we couldn't get it to restart. This aircraft had a history of being difficult to start in the hot, humid jungle conditions due to vapor lock. Vaporized fuel collected in the fuel line to the engine. The only solution was to open the line, turn on the electric fuel pump, and evacuate the vaporized fuel.

As we attempted this, something went terribly wrong. Spilled fuel in the engine compartment ignited, and flames burst from the engine compartment and quickly spread, licking at our feet in the cabin. The brake lines melted, and the brake fluid accelerated the fire. Only Don's quick thinking saved the aircraft from complete destruction. Grabbing the fire extinguisher and trying to subdue the flames, he yelled to some curious Quichua spectators, who always gathered when a plane was present. They brought cooking pots filled with water from a nearby ditch, and the fire was controlled.

Gervacio, Quichua pastor and school teacher at Limoncocha jungle center (Ecuador)

Meeting the Waorani (Auca) people

1960-1962

During my visits, I met Dayuma, the first Waorani (Auca) believer. I met Rachel Saint, Nate Saint's sister. (The Waorani called her "Star" in their language.) Dayuma and Rachel had patiently shared the gospel with the Waorani over many months, and one by one they believed. The two women labored together to translate the first Scriptures into the Waorani language. I met five of the six Waorani warriors who had killed the missionaries. I met Kimo, Minkaye, Nimonga, Dyuwi, and Gikita (Dayuma's uncle). Old Uncle Gikita became a believer when he realized that the guns that Nate and his companions were firing in the air could easily have taken his life. He then understood that the missionaries gave their lives so that the Waorani men could live.

I came to know and love old Uncle Gikita. He was the oldest of the men who speared the missionaries. He was the one who kept after the younger warriors until he was sure that all five men were dead. He died a few years ago, an old man in his eighties, with this testimony on his lips:

"When we were rushing at the men with spears, Nate had a gun in his hand, and he could have easily killed me in self-defense. But, instead, he shot in the air to try to scare us off rather than taking my life. He gave his life for me… We thrust our spears through the chest or back and killed them all, but when I later learned that they had come to share Christ's love with us, I was amazed. No Waorani would *ever* give his life in exchange for someone else's. That was the thing that got me thinking about a relationship with God. Now that I'm a believer, when I die and go to heaven, I'm going to look up Nate Saint and the others, and we are going to throw our arms around each other, and together we are going to live with Jesus forever."

I stood there, amazed by the power of the gospel. Just a few years before, we would have been targets, the objects of Waorani spears, because the Waorani were among the most violent people group on earth. If anyone ventured into their territory, they would be found later with multiple spears through their bodies. Now I stood around talking to the very people who had murdered missionaries while I was a student at Moody. There they were, no longer carrying wooden spears, but instead they were armed with the Sword of the Spirit, the Word of

God.

Rachel Saint lived in a house built by the Waorani. The houses in the village were made of jungle materials. They usually had a dirt floor, bark walls (if walls at all). I'm not sure I would want to live in the jungle in a home without walls. That could get really interesting because the jungle is full of creatures that hunt at night. Each home contained a roof structure created with rows of neatly aligned palm leaves. They were tied on one row at a time to keep the roof from being blown off during the strong jungle winds and storms. The people wove hammocks from the palm fiber. They slept in the hammocks, usually without blankets. If they felt cold, they would hang their feet out over the coals, trusting circulation to warm them up.

We came in with boxes containing strange objects that the people of the village had never seen before. They lined up on the porch and looked through the screens to see what peculiar things we had brought to Rachel. It was fun to arrive at mealtime. We ate jungle meat such as tapir. (I hoped it wouldn't be monkey). We might also have boiled or fried bananas. It was pleasant to just relax in the hammock and enjoy the jungle fare.

On one occasion, I had the privilege of flying Elizabeth Elliot and her daughter, Valerie, along with Mary Lou McCully and Barbara Youdarian, to the Waorani village. Here were three of the wives meeting the people that had made them widows and killed the father of Valerie. It was amazing that the women would even want to meet the people who had killed their husbands. Elizabeth stayed in the village with Valerie for a couple of years alongside Rachel. Then she came to the States, remarried, and entered a different type of ministry. Rachel and Nate's brother, Phil, missionary to Argentina, also came to meet the people that had killed his brother. I had the opportunity to fly him and a photographer out to the village.

Forrest with (l. to r.) converted killers, Dyuwi, Nimonga, Kimo, Minkaye, Gikita, vicious killer Dabu. and three unidentified young men

As the Waorani Christians began reading the newly translated Scriptures, they learned that believers are baptized. They said, "We're believers now, and we want to be baptized!" Rachel asked, "Who would you like to do your baptism?" They thought for a while, and they decided on Dr. Ev Fuller from the HCJB Hospital in Shell Mera, who had treated them on several occasions. I had the privilege of flying into Shell Mera, picking up him and his hospital administrator, and taking them out to the village. I was the official photographer for the initial Waorani baptism of the first eleven believers. They gave their testimonies before they went into the water. Although I couldn't understand their words, I could tell from the expressions on their faces and the enthusiasm in their voices that the Lord had wrought a real miracle in their lives.

The Waorani built a two-story church building. They met on the second floor because the ground floor was inhabited by their pets: dogs, pigs, monkeys, and chickens. They not only met on Sundays, but during the week for Bible studies and worship, singing hymns in their own language that Rachel had translated or prepared for them. I was awed that, for the first time in their history, a people group was worshiping the one true God.

Hunting and fishing with the Waorani

1960-1962

During one of my flights to their village, Kimo and Minkaye invited me to go hunting. They hoisted their nine-foot blowguns and dart-holders on their shoulders. I followed with the airplane survival shotgun in case these capable hunters needed backup. (*Not likely!*) They listened carefully to the sounds of monkeys in the tall trees. They could tell the size and species of their prey and could reproduce their language. This sometimes led to the curious monkeys giving away their hiding place in order to see who was calling, and afforded the hunters a shot. The hunters were accurate and could bring down game high in the jungle trees using darts tipped with curare, a potent anesthesia famous throughout the jungle. The big howler monkey, about the size of a small child, provided their favorite

His Faithfulness Reaches to the Skies

meat, which they would roast over an open fire or boil in a large pot.

As Rachel Saint focused on the translation of the Scriptures and a soon-to-be published book about the progress of the Gospel among the Waorani people, she brought her translation assistant, Dayuma, converted killer Kimo, and his wife, Dawa, to our jungle center, Limoncocha, where we resided.

We decided to invite them to go fishing on our jungle lake, replete with piranhas, alligators. electric eels, stingrays, and boa constrictors. From the safety of a fiberglass boat, the three Aucas, Margaret, and I embarked on the trip. The old, tired outboard motor sometimes cooperated, and at other times refused to start. No problem—we took paddles in case of trouble.

Communication in the boat proved interesting as we understood no Waorani, and they understood almost no Spanish. Dayuma was our go-between, understanding limited Spanish.

As the afternoon progressed, the Auca couple heard Margaret and me communicate in English and noticed repetition of the word "Honey," when I referred to Margaret. They questioned Dayuma as to the meaning of the term.

Dayuma tried to think of a word in their language that could convey the proper meaning. Finally, she came up with "Naa."

Later, we learned from Rachel that "Naa" was the term of endearment from the total word meaning, "favorite wife." That was a great discovery and wonderful translation, for indeed Margaret was very dear to me, and in fact, was also my one-and-only and favorite wife, my "dear one."

Later, they began to refer to our baby daughter, as "Naanita." You guessed it. It meant "little dear one."

Margaret and Anita at Auca-Waorani village, with Rachel Saint and Dayuma; converted killer Kimo in background

Anita visits the Waorani

1962

When Anita was still a baby, I flew her and Margaret to visit the Waorani people. Anita was about the age where she would jump into the arms of anyone who offered. When we went to the village, one of the grandmothers wanted to hold her, and Anita jumped into her arms. This grandmother took her around the village and introduced her to everyone. They were fascinated to see this light- skinned baby, probably the first one that many of them had ever seen. It was a beautiful feeling to be able to entrust the lives of my wife and my baby daughter to people that a few years before would have taken great delight in spearing us.

Family visit to Waorani village. (R. to L.) Margaret and Anita with Dayuma, husband Komi, Kimo. and unidentified young Waorani

The president's visit

1960-1962

"The president of Ecuador is coming to visit our mission center in the jungle," we were told. Wow! This had never happened before! His particular interest was to meet a Waorani, now that several had become Christians. They had stopped their savage killings with hardwood spears, but they still had a worldwide reputation from the killing of the five missionaries in 1956.

Dr. José María Velasco Ibarra was elected president of Ecuador for an unprecedented six times. A wonderful orator, he once boasted, "Give me a balcony in every town, and I'll win the election." He moved the emotions and hearts of his people with colorful speeches, full of rhetoric, and with his brilliant use of the Spanish language.

On the trail to the presidency, this story emerged about him: Dr. Velasco was speaking from the balcony in a small town. With an upraised hand pointing to the sky, he promised. "If you elect me, I'll get your town a bridge." Someone whispered, "But we don't have a river." He then raised his voice and said, "I'll get you a river, too."

Although he was a great speaker, he was also known for his almost completely bald head. As a result, he became the object of unkind jokes. Writers compared his head to a "papaya," a smooth head-shaped delicious tropical fruit.

Preparations for his visit included flying out to the Auca village, Tiwaeno, to bring in Kimo, a converted Waorani who participated in spearing the missionaries, his wife, Dawa, and Rachel Saint. Rachel would serve as interpreter for the President and the Auca visitors.

Rachel, Kimo, and Dawa were introduced to the President. Never having seen a bald person, Kimo's curiosity consumed him. He went to the President and rubbed his head! The President graciously allowed the surprising gesture, but later became quite serious. He asked Kimo, in Spanish, "What does Jesus Christ mean to you?"

Rachel translated the question into Waorani. Kimo's face brightened and he replied, "Jesus Christ is my Lord and Savior."

President of Ecuador, Dr. José María Velasco Ibarra and cabinet travel to the Wycliffe Jungle Center, Limoncocha. They meet Auca-Waorani Kimo, and wife Dawa. Kimo confesses his faith to the President.

Ecuadorians know the history of the Waorani (Auca) killings and consider this people group the lowest level of society. When their children are naughty, they call them *Auca*. As we witnessed the question and answer, and the miracle of Kimo's changed life, the power of the gospel became more impressive than ever—the lowest level of society giving testimony to the President of the country.

Later that evening, my wife, Margaret, and the other missionary wives prepared a jungle banquet for the President and his entourage. After dinner, the President rose to thank us for the visit and dinner. His speech included an unexpected affirmation of our mission work in his country. He used the line from the New Testament story of Mary and Martha, applying it to our labors in the jungle. "You have chosen the better part, which will not be taken from you."

Full circle

After 1962

In 1966 two Waorani believers attended and spoke at the Congress on Evangelism in Berlin, Germany. At the end, during the closing hymn, an African delegate could contain himself no longer. He jumped up on the platform, and hugged the Waoranis each in turn. It just about broke up the meeting. Kimo looked so surprised. But someone overheard one attendee say that the African delegate had just done what they all wanted to do.

Over the years Rachel began to lose her eyesight and could not continue the linguistic and translation work. Previously, two other Wycliffe missionaries, Rosie Jung from Wycliffe Germany and Cathy Peek from Wycliffe USA, had joined her in her work. They continued through 1992 and actually finished translating the New Testament. A bilingual school was built in the Waorani village.

In the mid-1990s, Margaret and I saw Rachel Saint at a missions conference in Wheaton, Illinois. She told us that when we share this story, we should tell people not to stop praying for the Waorani, because now that their borders are open, people are coming in with all kinds of temptations like alcohol and drugs. We need to pray that the Waorani will stay strong and true to the Word of God. Not all of the Waorani are Christians, and some of them still need to know the Lord.

After Rachel's death, the Waorani asked Steve Saint (son of missionary pilot Nate Saint) to come and live with them so he could be an intermediary between them and civilization, because they didn't know how to handle the outside world. So Steve and his family lived with them for a period of years. Until a serious accident limited his mobility, Steve made trips and took groups of people from the United States down to Ecuador to meet the Waorani. The visitors actually lived with the people in the village for short periods of time, experienced their way of life, and witnessed their spiritual transformation.

Over the years, not only did five of the surviving Waorani killers believe in Christ, but they also became pastors and spiritual leaders among their people. One of them, Minkaye, went on to travel with Steve Saint. With great spiritual fervor, he preaches to the unbelievers in our country. When he hears stories of the carnage of Columbine and other tragedies on high school and college campuses, Minkaye says that our society is just like theirs before Christ. He encourages Americans to stop the killing and to "follow God's trail" as the answer the Waorani have found in God's Word. Missionaries went to their country to take the Gospel to the Auca-Waorani. Now they come to our country to bring us the Gospel. Things have come full circle. Only God could orchestrate events like this.

Forrest Zander

I met Steve for the first time at a missions conference several years ago, where I was reunited with Minkaye and Tementa. It was a beautiful experience to see them with their spears and their blowguns and to know that now those were dedicated to the Lord, rather than being used for taking the lives of their enemies.

Steve Saint, Forrest, Tementa (leading Waorani evangelist), and Minkaye (Waorani warrior who speared Nate Saint) at Spiritual Emphasis Week at Wheaton Academy

The need for Bible translation

How would it be if, after you spent the better part of your life giving the Word of God to people, someone would come to you and say "thank you" for translating God's Word so that I could know Jesus? Now the next generation of Waorani children will not be wielding hardwood spears but rather, the Sword of the Spirit, the Word of God. We have no higher calling—whether working as translators or in some support capacity. Bringing the Word of God to a people group in a language they can understand empowers the transformation of lives, of cultures, of generations.

The Word of God in the mother tongue is transformational. Bible translation results in evangelism, church planting, and discipleship.

Chapter 4

FLYING IN COLOMBIA

A door opens in Colombia

1962-1964

One of the biggest challenges in missions is getting permission to enter a country. Many nations are closed to mission work.

When "Uncle" Cam Townsend, the founder of Wycliffe Bible Translators, first went to Mexico, it was a closed country. But God opened the door for him to make a friendship with President Lázaro Cárdenas.

This is how it happened. President Cárdenas came out to the Aztec village where Cam and his wife were working. The president noticed that the village was different. It was much more progressive. Buildings were painted. Fruit trees and gardens were planted. Drunkenness was declining.

The president investigated and discovered this gringo couple were living in the village, learning the language of the people, and translating the Bible. President Cárdenas became a guest in Uncle Cam's mobile home, a little old trailer that they had towed into town. When Cárdenas started to talk with Cam, he realized the reason for the progress he could see in the village.

He said, "Townsend, can you bring other young people to Mexico?"

"I'd be happy to, sir," Townsend replied, "if you can arrange for them to live in the country."

President Cárdenas agreed with one stipulation: "When you bring these young people in, please make sure that they also have a feeling for the physical and educational needs of the people."

Mary Johnson teaching reading to Secoya people in Ecuadorian jungles. Jungle flights provided transportation for the Johnson family and enabled them to translate the New Testament for the Secoya people.

That's how Uncle Cam formalized the concept of meeting the spiritual, educational, and physical needs of the people by translating the Scriptures, providing literacy training, and helping with community development, such as agricultural training programs and basic medicine.

Later this strategy opened the door in Colombia.

For many years, Colombia was off limits to Protestant missionaries. But when Uncle Cam was in Guatemala, he met an anthropologist who had just become the Director of Indian Affairs in Colombia. After this man learned what Uncle Cam had done in other countries, he said, "How can I get you people to come to Colombia?"

Uncle Cam gave him the condition: "If we can have a contract with the government that will allow us to help the people physically, educationally, and spiritually by translating the Bible, we will come."

That contract was signed in 1962.

At Uncle Cam's invitation, we said goodbye to Ecuador and moved to Colombia to set up a brand new aviation program.

Met at gunpoint

June 1964

Getting into Colombia was an adventure all by itself. It started on the banks of Lake Limoncocha in Ecuador. We gathered with our colleagues for a prayer of dedication. Then Margaret and I slipped and slid down the muddy banks to the waiting Aeronca Sedan float plane, with a friend carrying two-year-old Anita. The plane was a gift to the new field of Colombia from the Ecuador field.

His Faithfulness Reaches to the Skies

Aeronca 15AC Sedan on pontoons being lowered to the lake. We would later fly it to our new advance into Colombia.

Bill Eddy (right), Jungle Center Manager, wishing Margaret and Forrest "Godspeed" as they leave Ecuador for Colombia, 1964

Forrest Zander

Time for Colombia JAARS Flight #001! As I did my preflight inspection, it soon became evident that the plane wasn't going anywhere. It was tangled up in the lush vegetation at the water's edge. No problem. I took a canoe paddle to push us out further into the water. Unfortunately, the plant I was using for leverage gave way, and I fell into the lake. I climbed back onto the plane, stood on the float, took off my boots, and poured out the water.

Take two. I managed to get our ride to Colombia free from Ecuadorian entanglements. As I wrestled with the plane, our crowd of well-wishers standing under the hot tropical sun began to thin.

Free of all hindrances, the engine roared (well, choked) to life.

The Aeronca Sedan model 15AC, on floats, loaded, with just 150 hp and fixed pitch prop was quite difficult to get off the water. This old workhorse had seen many hours in the air. It was underpowered, a situation exaggerated by the weight of heavy floats.

However, when I got checked out in the Aeronca, I learned a special technique for getting this bird in the air. I added full power for take-off, pulled the stick all the way back into my stomach and held it there until the water line was as far back on the floats as possible, then started rocking the plane fore and aft until the floats began to emerge and plane on top of the water (like a speedboat). While doing this, I used the aileron control to pick one float off the water, while simultaneously correcting my course with the rudder pedals. As the aircraft began to pick up speed on the "step" and accelerate toward flying speed, I hoped to leave the surface of the earth before I ran out of lake. Of course, the heavier the load, the longer it took. No wind, high humidity, and hot temperatures made it even more difficult.

We were relocating from Ecuador to Colombia. We hoped to take some of our things with us. But as I tried to get airborne, it was clear we needed to lighten our load. After each unsuccessful takeoff attempt, we began unloading more baggage. Three times we returned to the bank to leave more and more of our possessions behind. The last thing we unloaded was a huge garment bag with our clothes. I began to wonder if I would need to leave my wife and daughter behind! But finally we were aloft. Cruising at 85 mph, I was grateful there was no headwind. If there had been, our ground speed would have been vastly decreased.

Anita was curled up between us asleep, as it was time for her afternoon nap.

We were en route to Colombia and a whole new adventure. There was just one problem. Unknown to us, Colombia wasn't expecting our arrival. The mission director in Colombia had asked the government officials to wire permission for us to land and to enter the country in the town of Puerto Leguízamo, which was home to a large naval base operated by the Colombian navy. Meanwhile, we had painted over the U.S. registry, N1400H, and had no Colombian registry as yet. We were in an airplane "without a country," painted red and white —the Peruvian military colors. To fully appreciate this, you must understand that Peru and Colombia had been at war twenty-three years earlier. Some of the suspicion and animosity remained.

On the ground, with a "foreign" aircraft circling the Navy base, the military personnel assumed this was a sneak attack from the country to the south. The war between Peru, Ecuador, and Colombia in 1941 was always on their minds. Colombia had lost expansive territories to Peru when the U.S. intervened and imposed a peaceful settlement during the throes of World War II. Backyard squabbles were not welcome with other formidable foes needing full attention. Hence the Navy base on the river dividing the countries, with ships on patrol, served to protect their borders from further annexation.

I landed on the Putumayo River, taxied into a small harbor carved out of the river bank, and approached a small pier. As I shut down the engine and exited the plane, I held the float to the pier as Margaret and baby Anita deplaned. Rope in hand, I began to tie the float to the pier.

Out of the corner of my eye, I noticed three men approaching us. Two carried guns, and they were trained on us. The third man was obviously a high ranking naval officer, the base commander. About this time, we began to figure out that the commander had no idea who we were and no notice that we would be arriving.

Interesting.

At least my pants were dry from falling into the lake a couple hours earlier.

I greeted the commander in Spanish, giving him my name, Forrest Zander. That didn't seem to help. "Forrest Zander" sounds strange and exotic to Spanish ears.

The commander abruptly pointed at Margaret, and said, "Como se llama ella?" (What is her name?)

In my best Spanish, I replied, "Margarita Maria."

Pointing to baby Anita, the commander asked her name.

"Ana Maria."

This was working a little better. At least Margaret and Anita's names had translatable equivalents familiar to Spanish ears. The commander relaxed, and the guns were lowered as I reached for our passports. He was grateful to meet Americans, esteemed at the time as friends of his country.

The commander introduced himself as Capitán Eduardo Melendez. He turned out to be the Supreme Commander of the Southern Naval Forces. I met with him in his office and explained the purpose of our mission and use of the aircraft. When I requested an official and legal entry into the country, he was happy to sign and stamp our passports. I inquired about the telegram from our mission office in the capital city, Bogotá, and found that it never arrived.

That explained a lot.

At the commander's instruction, we were escorted to the base officers' guest house. For the next several days, we enjoyed meals at the officers' mess: three meals a day consisting of small portions of boiled potatoes, rice, manioc, and a tiny piece of meat, and of course coffee or *gaseosa* (pop).

I left the family at the navy base and, with fuel donated by the

Colombian navy, made two flights to the south to pick up four linguists already in two language areas. I flew the four of them to the navy base. Then rain kept us pinned down for several days.

We had left our extra clothes in Ecuador. Our linguists had only their village attire. But Saturday night came, and with it, the dance and social event of the year. We were graciously invited and included in the planning. A babysitter and an early supper were provided for baby Anita. The wives of the officers had spent the day in anticipation of the evening. Some came from Bogotá with the latest fashions and most modern hairstyles. The six of us didn't quite "measure-up." We were definitely "fish out of water." Once the evening was underway, Margaret muttered that she was going to check on the baby. Pretty soon, all six of us left to "check on the baby," and never quite made it back to the dance.

A few days later we all caught a Colombian Air Force plane to Bogotá, leaving the Aeronca tied up at the navy base. It was soon evident that the Aeronca was not the plane for the operation in Colombia. A new Helio Courier arrived in July as a gift from friends in Illinois and Indiana. A second pilot arrived in August. The aviation program was launched in Colombia.

Later we were able to sell the Aeronca and used the funds to build a hangar for our growing fleet of planes. In the meantime, I found the U.S. World Air Charts (WAC) navigational maps to be inaccurate. Based on succeeding flights to the jungles, we later redrew them for the Colombia geodetic agency.

His Faithfulness Reaches to the Skies

By the way, the base commander became a good friend and transported our fuel to several points along the rivers in southern Colombia without cost. Later he became commanding admiral of the whole navy.

Provision from the sky

1964

In the early days of our air program in Colombia, finding fuel for the return flights from remote jungle areas presented a special challenge. Our friendship with the Commander of the Southern Forces of the Colombian Navy helped immensely. I took him up on his offer to use his ships to deliver aviation fuel to selected points along the tributaries of the Amazon River that flowed through southeastern Colombia. But one area on the Caquetá River wasn't on his itinerary. The whole river encountered a rocky formation, and over the centuries cut its way through, forming a gorge with an impassable series of rapids and cascades.

The Commander explained how I could supply fuel to that area: hire a motorized dugout canoe to transport the fuel in 55-gallon drums to the top of the gorge. The canoe driver would throw the drums into the river above the falls. Since aviation fuel is lighter than water, they would float near the surface. They would bounce down the rocky waterway and end up at the bottom dented and badly beat up, but still floating. Twenty-nine out of the 30 survived the ordeal. Another person, hired for the job, would be ready at the foot of the gorge to retrieve the floating barrels in his canoe and deposit them at the nearest jungle airstrip, Araracuara.

With arrangements for the fuel delivery completed well ahead of time, I left with a translator family, the Waltons, for the three hour twenty minute flight to the Muinane language area.

This was my first flight with the new Helio Courier in Colombia across the equator, that imaginary line dividing the earth into Northern and Southern Hemispheres. My goal was to land among the Muinane people. But first we'd have to navigate vast areas of jungle for three hours with inaccurate air charts and unknown checkpoints. We climbed to seven thousand feet, confirming check points I had chosen from the maps: the start of a river, now just a small creek, barely visible from the air; then the confluence with another creek, making the river wider and easier to see.

The thick jungle in a few areas gave way to patches of thin scrub growth. Just what we would need in case of a forced landing. *Maybe we could actually make an emergency landing without serious damage to the plane,* I thought.

We left that river system and began what we called "a crossover." This was solid jungle with no rivers in sight. Crossovers made praying easy. And necessary. Especially the first time. After some fifteen minutes, we came to the welcome sight of a large river—the Apaporis River according to the map.

The year before, a missionary pilot had mistaken this river for another. He flew up the river expecting to find a town with an airstrip. He learned too late his mistaken location. Low on fuel, he landed on a gravel beach to avoid crashing in the jungle. After three days, he and his two passengers were located by a military pontoon plane that landed on the river and provided fuel for their escape.

Passing the Apaporis, we began another crossover. This one was longer. I strained my eyes to locate some checkpoint, hopefully the beginning of another river that would parallel our course for the next half hour. A line of communication in case of engine failure. We found the river, but no houses or signs of human habitation. If we survived a crash landing along its tree-filled banks, we would have to provide our own river transportation. I had no idea how to make a dugout canoe, but I had built a raft of balsa wood during our survival training in southern Mexico.

The river soon became wide and easy to follow. Next another large river flowed into it. Our refueling destination, Araracuara, soon became visible. Araracuara, a small clearing in the jungle, was the Alcatraz of the Colombian penal system. It was a prison of no escape. Located on the banks of the Caquetá River, surrounded by vast and dangerous jungles, Araracuara provided the only airstrip in this vast tropical region. Air travel was the only way in or out. Its location made it the ideal prison without walls.

As we flew over the airstrip carved out of a flat rocky knoll above the river, we saw the cataract. The huge river almost disappeared in places as it cut its way through the rock. The water bounced its way down an impassable series of waterfalls, then widened out into what seemed like a large lake.

Weeks before, I had arranged transportation of 30 steel drums of aviation fuel, destined for the river trip to Araracuara. A telegram to the prison warden requested his assistance. Surely the fuel had arrived by now. A motorized dugout canoe would take the drums 100 miles downriver to the top of the cataract. The canoe driver would throw the barrels into the river. Hopefully, most of them would survive the rocky waterfalls. Someone from the prison would collect the battered containers as they floated on the river and store them until our arrival.

As we flew over the airstrip to check it and the prevailing wind, we noticed a large cargo plane on the side of the runway. A World War II vintage C-46, this relic still used by airlines in Colombia, had a tragic ending. The night before, just before dark, the pilot attempted to land in a jungle storm. He lost control, skidded off the runway at high speed, and hit a pile of dirt and gravel. The aircraft came to a stop with such force that the landing gear collapsed and the motors were severed from the wings. It provided ample testimony to the hazards of jungle flying. Miraculously, the crew and passengers escaped unharmed.

After we landed, the prison warden and a handful of trusted inmates became our welcoming party. And then the bad news. Our fuel, necessary for the return flight, had not arrived. Now what would I do? Miles from nowhere, at or near the end of the world, and no fuel.

But the Lord had gone before us. I thought of the wrecked aircraft nearby. The wing tanks had to have enough fuel for a return flight to its base of operations. The warden took me to the village to meet the pilots. Still shaken by the accident, they gladly agreed for me to use as much fuel as I needed. They jokingly commented that they didn't plan to use it in the near future!

I parked our plane as close to the C-46 as possible. Equipped with my usual jungle refueling equipment, a five gallon bucket and hose, I siphoned the fuel from its huge wing tanks into the bucket. Yes! The welcome green-dyed 130 octane fuel entered the hose. Then I climbed up on the wing of our plane and poured the bucket of fuel through a filter into a funnel and into my wing tank. One bucket at a time soon became the thirty gallons of borrowed fuel I needed.

Only later did I realize this special provision from the Lord. And I remembered the words from the prophet Isaiah, "Before they call, I will answer, and while they are yet speaking, I will hear." (KJV)

A narrow escape

1964-1969

The refueling operation deep in the jungle was just about completed. I had just poured the last five gallons of high octane aviation fuel into the wing tanks of our mission plane. As I climbed down from the wing, a man smoking a lighted cigarette approached. Lying on its side, the still-open fifty gallon barrel invited disaster at the smallest spark.

Oblivious to the potential danger, the stranger removed the spent cigarette from his mouth. Before I could call a warning, he threw it right in front of the still open fifty-gallon barrel, now half-filled with volatile fumes and twenty gallons of even more dangerous aviation fuel. The cigarette landed in a puddle of spilled fuel that burst into flames. The flames licked at the opening. A fiery explosion could now happen at any moment.

The purpose of our flight was to resupply translators Jim and Jan Walton and their two small children with food and medicines. Located more than three hours' flight from our center of operations, their task was to learn the Muinane Indian language, formulate an alphabet, analyze the grammatical system, teach the people to read and write their own language, and translate portions of Scripture. They eagerly anticipated the day when God's Word would penetrate Muinane hearts, Muinanes would believe in Christ, and a vibrant church would be born in this solitary place.

History had not been kind to the Muinanes. During the rubber boom of the early 1900s, they numbered between five and ten thousand souls. Rubber hunters decimated them by bringing slavery, disease, mistreatment, and death to thousands. If they failed to bring in the required amount of latex from the wild jungle trees, they were punished severely. By the time the Waltons arrived to work in the tribe, only a few hundred survived, alone and almost forgotten by the world, but not by God.

The flight also served as a routine check for our new pilot, George. As chief pilot for our mission in Colombia, I was responsible to see that every new pilot could navigate safely over unknown terrain, find the tiny airstrips hidden deep in the jungles, land, then take off again safely. I also pointed out alternate airstrips along the route to use in case of inclement weather or mechanical problems. This flight took us across the equator into the Southern Hemisphere.

His Faithfulness Reaches to the Skies

In addition, on long flights like this one, I wanted to be sure George knew the locations of our gasoline storage facilities, how to access them, and the individuals who cared for them. Any fuel in the jungle, far from supply points, is a rare and valuable commodity. It could easily "disappear"—appropriated for use in outboard motors on the rivers or for cooking in small gas stoves in private homes. Because this round-trip flight was longer than the fuel carrying capacity of our small aircraft, refueling was necessary for the return flight home.

George was also learning quickly the hazards of missionary flight operations—like when cigarette-toting strangers appear out of nowhere during refueling.

As the flames licked at the open barrel, all the laws of physics dictated an explosion that would drench us with flaming fuel. We could be killed or badly burned.

I jumped down from the wing of the airplane. Giving the barrel a hard kick to roll it away from the burning puddle of fuel, I yelled to George and the two men who were helping us. We quickly pushed the airplane to a safe distance and capped the barrel as the burning puddle slowly extinguished itself. Miraculously, the explosion never occurred.

Why no explosion? How were our lives spared?

I believe the Lord's unseen hand or that of a guardian angel covered the barrel opening and prevented a fiery disaster. Someday, in heaven, we'll learn about the many occasions, known and unknown, when the Lord spared our lives to serve Him until our time is up. As someone once told me, "Christians are immortal, until the Lord calls us home."

Forrest Zander

No oil pressure

1964-1969

Taking off from a jungle airstrip, I customarily surveyed the instrument panel, checking for fuel and oil pressure. The oil pressure needle was fluctuating near zero. Emergency! Without oil, the engine would quickly overheat and stop. I quickly turned the aircraft and landed safely. Fortunately, we pilots are required to have an Airframe and Power Plant Mechanic license as well as a Commercial Pilot license. I quickly changed hats from pilot to mechanic. But I had never experienced engine oil pressure failure.

I radioed our Center and asked for Ed Svedberg, our Chief Mechanic. Ed was a crackerjack mechanic and knew airplane engines inside and out. I explained the problem to him, and he came up with a tentative solution. Sometimes small pieces of carbon get into the oil and can prevent the oil pressure relief valve from closing. I knew exactly where this valve was located. Grabbing the tool kit from under my seat, I disassembled the relief valve. Sure enough, there was the carbon. I cleaned it, ran up the engine, and the oil pressure needle was in the green range. I took off on a test flight with no passengers and all was normal. I was able to continue that series of flights far from our Center.

Thank the Lord for savvy mechanics and for takeoff procedures that catch problems before they become serious.

Engine stops at 7,000 feet

1964-1969

I was in the right Instructor seat and a new pilot, Ron, was in the left Pilot-in-Command seat. We were returning from a routine check at an airstrip which served the translators working with the Piapoco language group. Most of the flight was over plains country but interspersed with areas of solid jungle.

At 7,000 feet, the engine suddenly stopped. Emergency! Ron radioed the Center with our position and situation and expertly chose a flat area for a potential forced landing. We both surveyed the instrument panel and saw the problem: fuel starvation. One wing tank indicated empty and the other still half full. The tank with fuel was not draining into the header tank which then fed the engine. Why? As we descended, at about 4,000 feet, the engine suddenly roared to life. We were approaching an area of solid jungle. Ron climbed back up to a higher altitude in case the engine quit again. We were only about 20 minutes from home with no alternate airstrips along our route. The solid jungle would take perhaps 10 minutes to traverse. We would go halfway, and if the engine quit again before the mid-point, we would glide back to the plains. If we made it to the mid-point, we could glide to a flat area past the jungle. But the engine continued running normally, and we made it safely back to our Center.

Once again Chief Mechanic Ed figured out the problem. Inspecting the fuel cap on the wing tank that caused the malfunction, he noticed the rubber seal had a worn spot on it causing a leak to outside air. At our cruising altitude the reduced pressure or suction on the top of the wing near the fuel tank cap held the fuel in that tank, not allowing it to reach the engine. Only after we descended to a lower altitude where the pressure was less, was the fuel able to flow, making it possible for the engine to restart. Ed replaced the rubber seal and solved the problem.

No brakes!

1964-1969

Jungle flying required a rigid and detailed preventive maintenance program, minimizing the potential for serious problems. Even so, unforeseen difficulties arose.

Flying into the capital city of Bogotá required climbing to 12,000 feet on a clear day, and higher on a cloudy day, to safely clear the Andes Mountains. Bogotá is situated in a bowl-like valley at an elevation of 8,350 feet. I had a patient with a heart problem in the back, and I was landing with a new aircraft in a crosswind at Bogotá's El Dorado International Airport. The crosswind required heavy braking to keep the aircraft on the runway. However, as I applied the brakes, I noticed a very weak response. The crosswind prevailed, the aircraft entered a ground loop, and the wingtip dug into the pavement. Taxiing to the parking area, I wondered why the brakes had failed. A temporary repair on the damaged wingtip allowed me to return to the Center. Ed, the Chief Mechanic, figured it out. The wheels with brakes are identical. They were installed on the wrong sides. Instead of the rotation of the wheels enhancing the braking, the incorrect installation had the opposite effect, almost no braking. On short jungle runways, having no brakes would invite almost certain disaster. We had no idea that the brakes weren't working. But the crosswind caused the problem to manifest itself. Again, God protected us from a potentially fatal mechanical malfunction, and allowed us to find and correct the problem on time.

The "in house"

1964

Early in the development of the Lomalinda center of operations, Uncle Cam (William Cameron Townsend), the Founder and General Director of our mission, bought two dilapidated house trailers from an oil company. He arranged for them to be towed to Lomalinda as quick housing while the center was being developed. One trailer, home for his family, was installed in an area of jungle beside the lake.

Our director organized a Center Committee to define and regulate the buildings and permanent homes. I was appointed chairman of this committee and functioned when the committee was not in session. It fell to me to be sure the new regulations were being followed. One of those regulations stipulated that no outhouses were to be constructed; each home was to have indoor bathroom facilities with a septic system.

One day I was visiting with Uncle Cam at his trailer and realized there was an outhouse attached, a simple hole in the ground with a wooden seat over it, an outhouse by definition. Now what do I do? He was the Founder and General Director of a world-wide ministry. I was a lowly newcomer with limited authority and hopefully good judgment. I was torn between just letting it go or enforcing the rule. I decided to take a stab at talking to Uncle Cam about his outhouse. I explained the regulation in as diplomatic a way as possible. Cam retorted, explaining that this was not an "out" house. It was attached to his trailer; therefore, it was an "in" house.

Impasse! Happily, he had to be away for an extended period. The trailer would be occupied by another family. A septic tank was dug and a standard "in" house flush toilet became a fixture. Good, because my family would be the occupants while our permanent house was being constructed.

Who is this Jesus?

1965

Not all ministry occurred during flying events. During the first linguistic workshop held at Lomalinda in 1965, translators from several languages brought language assistants. They worked with a consultant to establish a working alphabet in each language. I had flown most of them to the workshop, and they became my friends. In addition to speaking their mother tongues, most of the assistants had at least a rudimentary ability in Spanish.

Burdened for their spiritual welfare, I invited them to a Bible study. All six of them came to study the Gospel of Mark with me. We used a popular Spanish New Testament written in simple vocabulary. The Holy Spirit was working in their hearts as we read and studied together.

Early days at Lomalinda Center: We ran the commissary. The 50 lb. catfish would be cut up and distributed to the few families at the center.

Those who came from jungle language groups knew firsthand the power of Satan and the fear that accompanied the rituals and spirit worship in their villages. Some of their very own family members were shamans who led the spirit worship. When they learned from Mark's Gospel of the power of Jesus over the demons and how they were powerless as Jesus cast them out, I could tell that the Scriptures were having an impact.

One particular Sunday, as we read about Jesus' power to work miracles, I asked, "Who is this Jesus?" Andres, from the Muinane language, son of the village chief, responded, "He is the Son of God." Andres became the first believer among the Muinane people.

Forrest with his Bible study group from five different tribes during a linguistic workshop at Lomalinda. Andres, beside Forrest, is the son of Capitán Fernando to whom Forrest delivered the pigs.

The Cuiba

1968

During my years in Colombia, Wycliffe reached out to the Cuiba, a primitive and nomadic people group living in the northeast plains country. The Cuiba had no villages and no crops. They subsisted on meat from hunting. Their only food was charred meat cooked over an open fire. Mothers often lost their ability to nurse their babies, and as a result, few survived. Sickness was rampant. No medicines were available. Some nearby ranchers hunting on horseback entertained themselves by shooting any Cuiba they met with high powered rifles. They considered the Cuiba to be animals. All of this pushed the Cuiba people to the verge of extinction.

Enter Marie and Isabel, both trained nurses and linguists, called to give the Word of God to the Cuiba in their own language. Much of their early time was invested in treating the sick, particularly the children. They introduced powdered milk and vitamins, and taught them to plant and harvest more nutritious food, build houses from available materials, and start living in villages to facilitate farming and schooling. Eventually a number of Cuiba took our agricultural training in crops and animals.

As the team studied the language, they discovered there was no word for God. Somehow Isabel and Marie were able to communicate God's love by learning the language, serving the people, and meeting their basic needs. Their language helper, Weinacu, and his wife, Camna, became believers. Weinacu had a real burden for the spiritual welfare of his people. He eventually became the first pastor and school teacher in the village.

Isabel and Marie are among my heroes, spending many years ministering to the Cuiba. In spite of cerebral malaria and other health concerns, these ladies lived the Acts of the Apostles before our very eyes. As a result of their labors, many Cuiba completed elementary school in their village. Some went on to complete high school, university, and returned to serve the Cuiba as school teachers, doctors, health promoters, pastors, and evangelists.

When the team needed a break, we flew them to Lomalinda for respite from the primitive tribal living. Getting in and out of Cuiba territory sometimes created some tense moments in the air. At the height of the rainy season, all the rivers flooded their banks. There was water everywhere. I felt like I was flying over the ocean. If the engine quit, there was only an occasional island of high ground, and most of those "islands" contained houses or other features that would make landing impossible. If the engine quit, we would be in serious trouble. I was always happy to make it to the all-weather airstrip they developed in Cuiba territory that was high enough to escape the flood.

Once Isabel and Marie arrived in Lomalinda, they were able to live in their small house on a vacant lot next to us, with an additional house for the Cuiba family who usually accompanied them to continue translation work.

Tabchi was one of the Cuiba who accompanied the team to Lomalinda. When not helping with language work, Tabchi worked for us cutting our lawn with his machete. There were no lawn mowers in those days. He appreciated the chance for added income. When our son Alby was a small tot, he watched Tabchi working and followed him around, imitating his machete strokes with a stick. Alby told us that when he grew up he wanted to be just like Tabchi. We bought him a toy plastic machete so he could realize his dream.

Our children: Alby, Arlene and Anita

We learned to love the Cuiba, and Margaret frequently invited them to share a meal with us. Food literally disappeared from our table as their voracious appetites took over. They were especially enamored with her delicious chocolate cakes.

One day Margaret discovered a snake under the dining table in the living room. She screamed at the top of her lungs for help. Everyone came running. Weinacu arrived with his bow and arrows, and he shot the snake on the floor under the lace tablecloth. The arrow went right through the table cloth and nailed the snake underneath it. From then on the tablecloth had a big hole in it. There was no easy way to replace the tablecloth, so I'm not sure whether Margaret was happy because the snake was dead or sad because her tablecloth was ruined.

But it was a joy to know Isabel and Marie, true apostles to the Cuiba. It was an honor to provide air transportation for them, to know them as friends, and to enjoy members of their tribe as neighbors. Isabel and Marie will receive a great reward, and heaven will be richer as the Cuiba will be represented in that "great throng which no man could number" from every tribe and language, each praising the Lord Jesus in his or her very own language. I hope I can find the "Cuiba Corner" in heaven and join them.

Snakes

The jungle and plains were inhabited by many types of snakes. Some were venomous, and without anti-venom serum a bite could be fatal. The tiny coral snake was the most deadly. There was no remedy for its venom. Its sting causes death in about three hours. A missionary on our center encountered a coral snake in his house. He went after it with a stick. The snake aggressively came after him before he successfully killed it.

In addition to the snake killed by Weinacu, the Cuiba Indian, we encountered several other snakes over the years. We killed a four-foot snake in one of the bedrooms, coiled between the rafters. He had come in through a hole in the screen window.

Rattlesnakes up to five or six feet in length were common on our center in Colombia. One day Margaret was walking from our home in the jungle on a well-used pathway. Baby Arlene, at eighteen months, was toddling behind her. Apparently a large rattler was sleeping in a sunny spot beside the path. Startled, it awakened and struck at Margaret, missing her leg, but brushing against it as it plopped into the brush and disappeared. The baby was a few steps behind her and could easily have been its victim. The incident reminded us of the care of our loving Father in Heaven.

Stung!

1961

One day while working in the garden, I was stung on a finger by a conga ant, a large bug about an inch long, well documented to have one of the most intense insect bites of the entire animal kingdom. Its sting caused excruciating pain lasting several hours. It hurt so badly I could do nothing but suffer. Nothing seemed to alleviate it. I have never in all my life experienced pain so intense.

In addition to stinging insects, there were other pests. Cockroaches were a constant menace. They tended to overrun the kitchen. Oh, my! We caught baby Arlene with a big one in her mouth. Sugar ants also infested the kitchen, and leaf cutting ants carried away entire bushes in a very short time.

12' by 20' cabin, our first home at Lomalinda

Helio Couriers in hangar at Lomalinda

Running out of fuel

1964-1969

Copilot Ron and I watched the fuel gauges carefully as we crossed the Andes Mountains in Colombia in our new missionary plane. Having inaugurated a new airstrip in the western foothills, we were headed home after being absent from our families for several days.

We were cruising at 16,000 feet—high enough to clear the mountains in that area. To stay alert and alive at that altitude, we used oxygen masks. This maiden flight of our new aircraft allowed us to test the turbo-charged engine, oxygen system, and amount of fuel the engine would use at this unfamiliar altitude. The tanks were full when we took off, but as we studied the needles on the fuel gauges, we could see that they were going down much faster than anticipated.

This was a problem.

We still had the last of three ranges of the Andes to cross before we could descend to a lower altitude where the engine would consume less fuel. We did some rapid calculations. It was way too risky to try to fly all the way home. We needed to refuel.

But where? The closest commercial airport was far, far away. Alternate airstrips were scarce in this remote area, much less airstrips with fuel.

Clearing the highest mountain peaks and passing the foothills on the eastern side, we quickly descended to preserve fuel and looked for a place to land. Then we found it—an airstrip we had noticed earlier, right at the foot of the mountain. But what about fuel? Would they have any? We didn't know, but we needed to commit, and there were no other good options. If they had no fuel, we would need to call our home base for the other pilot to bring us enough fuel to get home. Costly, but cheaper than running out of fuel and crashing our new plane.

Circling the airstrip to check for wind direction and obstacles, we spotted about twenty barrels. They were painted blue, indicating 91/98 octane aviation grade fuel! We also saw a contingent of Colombian army soldiers waiting for us. This remote airstrip could easily be used to refuel aircraft flying drugs to the USA. And we could be mistaken for drug runners. We had no choice but to land.

Identifying ourselves to the army commander, and surrounded by his troops, we explained our presence and our need for fuel. The commander told us that the airstrip was used for petroleum exploration. Normally the oil company helicopter refueled here. Yes, the barrels were full, and yes, we could have the 30 gallons we needed, free!

As we finished refueling, a black cloud and storm approached. Too late to escape before the storm hit, we fled with the troops to a protected area. As we conversed with the commander, we realized that here was a captive audience, a mission field, and the Lord had arranged our fuel problem and the storm. As the rain pattered on the roof, we read passages from our Spanish New Testament.

When we finished, the rain stopped. We asked the commander if he had a New Testament. His answer, no. Gift in hand, he

121

promised to read it to his troops in the days ahead and even have a Bible study with them. We thanked the commander profusely for the fuel. Then joyfully, we departed, realizing again that our times are in the Lord's hands. Sometimes delays and problems are His way of opening doors to new opportunities to love people and to serve Him.

Tropical rainstorm over the jungle

Trouble at 4,000 feet

1964-1969

The Muinane people lived deep in the Amazonian jungles of Colombia, just south of the equator. Their lives had been decimated by disease, enslavement, and loss of hope. Adding to their difficult existence, their main source of protein from fishing and hunting was in short supply.

Jim and Jan Walton, with their two small children, began living in their village. I had the joy of flying the Walton family to the village and supplying them with food and medicines in our small single engine aircraft.

On one of the early flights to Muinane territory, I discovered that the food shortage existed. I proposed to Jim that we introduce pig raising and infuse a regular source of protein to the area. Jim agreed it was worth a try, but where would we get the pigs? A nearby prison colony just 22 minutes flying time away seemed to hold the answer.

Landing at the prison colony, I located the warden, and bought a male and female pig. They brought the squealing pigs, their feet bound with jungle vines, to the airplane. What if they became untied or the vines broke? The warden assured me they were "strong vines." I put the pigs in the back of the plane, behind the pilot seat, and took off.

At 4,000 feet, on a heading for the Muinane village, I turned to check on my piggy passengers. To my surprise one of the pigs was loose. It seemed he wanted to become my copilot. I knew his flight training was inadequate, so I kept him at bay with one hand as I flew the correct compass course with the other. Soon he settled down behind me.

A few minutes later, I checked again. Both of them were untied! Now they wanted to take over the pilot *and* copilot seats. What should I do? Solid jungle beneath me and at least ten minutes to the nearest airstrip. I kept them both at bay with one hand and guided the plane toward the Muinane village.

Fortunately, the pigs determined that my flying skills surpassed theirs, and they allowed me to land safely.

I delivered the pigs to Chief Fernando, who would raise the

first litter, and soon, according to our plan, hand off a male and female to the next family. That family would do the same, and soon the entire village would be in business.

Muinane Chief, Capitán Fernando, with pigs, loose at 4,000 feet, safely delivered

But things did not work out as planned. One pig died. The other became Muinane pork chops. On the surface, it seemed that our plan had failed. But, no! The Waltons had come to show the love of Jesus to the Muinane people. Our pig project demonstrated that love in a practical way.

The Waltons lived with the Muinanes, demonstrating that love for some eighteen years, translated God's Word for them, and a number believed in Christ.

Years later, Arturo told me that just before the Waltons came to their village, they had lost all hope. They had decided to have no more children and just disappear off the face of the earth. The Waltons' arrival and ministry preserved a people group, the Muinane, from extinction. Some will be in heaven with us, worshiping the Lamb.

No airstrip—no problem

1964-1969

One of the most beautiful places on earth, the llanos (plains) of eastern Colombia begin at the foot of the Andes Mountains. The flat lands gradually decline in elevation from some 900 feet above sea level and finally arrive far to the East at the Orinoco River bordering Venezuela. Rich grasslands feed thousands of cattle on vast ranches, interspersed with low rolling hills and streams with jungle vegetation along their borders. Indian tribes speaking different languages live in small villages and depend on hunting wild pigs, tapir, monkeys, and other wild game that inhabit the jungle areas. Fish of many tropical varieties also provide food: from small caribe (piranha) to huge catfish weighing up to several hundred pounds.

Although cattle are branded to ensure ownership, most land is free-range to allow the cattle to find their food. Cattle are rounded up at times by the vaquero (cowboy) owners and transported by truck or river to market towns. The larger ranches have an airstrip for the use of more wealthy owners, which are serviced by charter flights on mostly single engine aircraft. Sometimes referred to as the "Texas" of South America, this area exports beef to markets throughout the continent.

His Faithfulness Reaches to the Skies

Flying over the llanos in support of Bible translators was anything but easy. During the rainy season vast areas flood, some hundreds of square miles in area, with little high ground adequate for a forced landing. During dry season, ranchers renew the grassland by setting fire to the dry grasses. As the rainy season draws near, succulent new grass provides food for the roaming cattle. In the meantime, visibility in the air is reduced to almost zero and navigation is difficult. The smoke and haze sometimes rise to 7,000 feet until the rainy season cleanses the atmosphere. Then the storm fronts invade the land bringing low visibility and chubascos (vicious windstorms), which make flying dangerous or impossible. Between fronts, the visibility is clear and unlimited, mostly in the mornings. Later in the day, solar heating creates storm clouds and more hazards.

One day, flying in support of Bible translators located in the llanos about two hours east of our center, I was well into the flight when a storm blocked further progress. I hated to return all the way home and waste the flight hours with their associated costs of fuel, insurance, and other expenses. Before the storm moved in to my present position, I spotted a thatch-roofed house at a small ranch. There were tracks in the grass where a truck had been recently, probably to supply the rancher and truck cattle to market. I surveyed carefully an area that looked promising. No, it wasn't an airstrip, but there was plenty of length for landing and takeoff and no obstacles to contend with. And no one seemed to be home at the time. Electing to land quickly and weather the storm on the ground, I remembered the aviation lore that "it is better to be on the ground wishing you were up there, than to be up there, wishing you were on the ground but not finding a place to land." Soon the weather cleared and I was able to complete my mission for the day.

Whoops, wrong country!

1964-1969

One of the most interesting aspects of those early years of starting and unrolling a sound aviation program was flying survey to discover where the Indian tribes were located, what language they spoke, and if they needed a written language and Bible translation. We had heard about an elusive Indian group called the Carabayo located somewhere in the northeastern llanos (plains). The area was cattle country with large ranches about 5–10 minutes flying distance apart and many with operable airstrips. Two translator-linguists and I had the intriguing job of trying to locate the Carabayo. Landing at the first airstrip and questioning the owner and his ranch hands, we learned that this was not on their priority list. Yes, they had heard of the Carabayo, no they didn't live nearby, but try over there. They would point in a particular direction, so we would take off and look in that area. Not finding any signs of Indian houses or clearings, we would land at the next ranch and inquire. I didn't count how many ranches we stopped at, always with the same answers. Toward afternoon with success eluding us, we spotted a larger ranch with a nice airstrip somewhere along the Arauca River. We stopped there and asked the name of the ranch. It wasn't a ranch, and the name was Puerto Nino, Venezuela. Whoops, big mistake. The river was the dividing line, but we thought we were still in Colombia. We had no permission to land in the neighboring country and would be in big trouble, probably mistaken for drug runners or some type of smugglers. I quickly urged my passengers back into the plane and made a dash for the end of the runway for takeoff. As we broke ground, we saw a military jeep with uniformed men headed our way. Whew! Narrow escape and international incident averted! And we never did find the Carabayo.

Aerial survey team, (L. to R.) Pilot Ron Ehrenberg, Linguist-Translators John Waller and Stan Schauer, Pilot Forrest Zander

Capitán Fori

1964-1969

I was the first pilot to begin air service to the Piapoco people in the eastern grasslands of Colombia. Vast areas in the east are devoid of trees, making any relatively flat area a potential landing strip. To create an airstrip, the local people simply cut the tall grass or burned it off during the dry season and marked the two ends and side boundaries. In this way, the translators in the survey party were able to lay out an airstrip that soon became operational beside the village.

When I arrived, the Piapocos learned my title and name was Capitán Fori (Forrey). Soon after, a new Piapoco baby was born and given the legal name Capitán Fori. I wonder if they referred to the little boy growing up as Capitán or Fori or both. But it was a great honor to have a namesake among my indigenous Piapoco friends.

Malaria

1964-1969

Living in the tropics has many pros, but there are also some cons. Malaria is one of them. We all took prophylaxis to prevent it, but somehow Margaret and I came down with it anyway. We felt like we were up in the arctic one moment, and down on the equator the next. The chills were terrible. We couldn't get warm enough with all the blankets in the house. It hit in cycles. Just when it seemed like it was going away, it came back and hit us all over again. Even with treatment, it took a long time to recover.

A near disaster

1964-1969

There's no such thing as a long airstrip in the jungles of Colombia. When conditions are optimal, landing and taking off are tricky—there's no margin for error. If anything goes wrong, things become dangerous very quickly.

His Faithfulness Reaches to the Skies

My new missionary pilot colleague, Ron, and I had just landed on a new airstrip the day before. We were there to commence air service to Bible translators just beginning their work among the Barasano people, a tribe located deep in the Amazon rainforest, not far from the Brazilian border. Air service allowed us to not only bring in much needed medical and other supplies, but also to shuttle in the translator's wife and children. Flights in and out allowed Ron to pick up valuable training and experience in jungle flying.

Our mission complete, we accelerated down the runway to take off. As we approached the end of the airstrip, the aircraft should have jumped into the air as I eased the controls back for liftoff. But it didn't want to fly. It felt heavy and sluggish. The stumps and fallen trees at the end were getting closer. What was wrong?

The airplane, a few yards from the nearest stumps at runway's end, should fly. I hauled back hard on the controls. The plane hesitated, then reluctantly staggered into the air like a sick bird. We cleared the first big stumps and fallen trees. It refused to gain altitude. It began to settle into the debris. I heard the wheels begin to clip dry branches. Another few inches of lost altitude and CRASH!

But we picked up a few miles per hour of air speed as we settled. Just enough to fly above the low obstacles.

Now the real test began. Fast running out of airspace over fallen trees and stumps, we had tall jungle trees ahead.

I leveled the plane and aimed right for them.

The plane gained a little more speed.

Then, just before hitting the trees, I pulled hard on the controls, and we flared up over them to a safe altitude.

Whew!

In the safety of a normal climb out, we analyzed the near disaster. As we circled the airstrip and looked at the wind indicator, we knew. The red rag ribbon on the pole beside the airstrip showed wind blowing from the opposite direction!

We had started the takeoff with a headwind. During the takeoff run, the wind switched to a dangerous tailwind. But, once again, the gentle care of our loving Savior had preserved our lives. "For great is your love, reaching to the heavens; your faithfulness reaches to the skies" Psalm 57:10 NIV

Saved by the storm

1964-1969

My copilot Ron and I flew a missionary Bible translator and his supplies into a remote and rugged jungle area located in the western foothills of the Andes Mountains in Colombia—one of the rainiest places of the world. The annual rainfall can top 400 inches. This was the first time we ever used this airstrip. What we didn't know—until we landed—was that the heavy rainfall on the surrounding mountains drained into this little valley and created a gigantic mud puddle.

The moment we touched down, we knew we had made a mistake. The airplane sank up to the axles in mud.

His Faithfulness Reaches to the Skies

We were stuck!

Trained at Moody Bible Institute, in the finest missionary aviation school in the world, I was taught to take off from soft, wet airstrips. But none as soft and muddy as this one.

Sometimes jungle airstrips get a bit muddy. Solution: find a rain shower for a mid-air wash.

This was not a good situation. There were no good options. On one hand we could take the airplane apart and hire workers to carry it out piece by piece. The walk to the nearest road would take several hours. We then would need to hire a truck to make the long, expensive trip back to our center of operations for reassembly.

On the other hand, we could try to fly it out. Here's the catch: We might not work up the speed needed for lift off, which would guarantee a crash.

We weighed the options and decided to attempt a takeoff. After unloading the missionary and his cargo, apologizing for planning never to return, we boarded the aircraft.

If the airplane couldn't approach takeoff speed as we neared the end of the runway, we would cut the power and settle back into the mud. But if our airspeed gauge indicated near takeoff velocity, I would try to pull it out of the mud. Ron would carefully adjust the engine turbocharger for maximum power, while I piloted the aircraft.

We started the engine and looked down the short runway. Anything could happen.

Bowing our heads, we prayed. "Lord, help!" What else could we say? We felt like the disciples on the Sea of Galilee.

As we lifted our eyes from that prayer, there was the answer in the sky right in front of us. A big black rain cloud came boiling over the nearest ridge. And as that storm approached, the wind began to blow, and blow hard, right down the runway. Exactly what we needed!

Ron applied power to the engine, and the plane just sat in the mud, vibrating from the surge of power. Then the wind began to provide lift to the wings, lightening the load on the landing gear. The wheels began to turn slowly and plow mud. The lift on the wings increased as we slowly crept down that runway. Which would come first, the end of the runway or takeoff velocity?

I watched the airspeed indicator creep forward, and, as we neared the end of the runway, I pulled back on the controls.

His Faithfulness Reaches to the Skies

The aircraft staggered out of the mud.

Unstuck! Airborne!

Whew!

We climbed out of that steamy valley and dodged the storm. As we set our course for home, our hearts filled with thanksgiving. The same Lord who calmed the storm on the sea and saved the disciples' lives, sent us a storm just when we needed it and rescued us from a difficult situation.

We all face challenges in life where it seems like there are no good options. I am glad that we serve a God who can make a way for us, even when we're stuck up to the axles in mud.

A successful hunt

1967

The missionary kids in Lomalinda urgently needed more room in their school. To meet that need, four men from central Illinois traveled to Colombia. One was a highly skilled professional brick layer. The four worked hard and put up the building in record time.

As we got to know them at mealtimes and in the evenings, it was evident they were sportsmen, hunters and fishermen. As an expression of appreciation, I invited them to fly with me to a remote area of the jungle where, hopefully, fish and game would be abundant. We only had one day and had to make the most of it.

We landed at an abandoned airstrip, rarely used at that time.

There we were met by three local hunters who were camped there and looking for jaguars (*tigre* in Spanish), prized for their beautiful skins. A skin would bring a high price when taken to civilization.

This was an unexpected treat. We could hunt with local guides! We agreed on a price and also offered to contribute any game we bagged to their food supply.

We split into three teams. Two of our guests went off in one direction with one of the guides, the other two guests went in another with a second guide, and I set off with the third guide, a man named Luis.

Luis and I walked for a long time. His skill at detecting animals gave me a chance to bring them down. I killed a couple of howler monkeys and a wild turkey. Satisfied with our part of the hunt, we started back to the airstrip carrying our game in a bag Luis had carefully woven out of jungle materials.

As we headed back, the mid-afternoon heat left us hot and sweaty. When we came to a beautiful shade tree, we decided to pause and catch our breath.

At that moment, the Holy Spirit prompted me to share my faith with Luis. After explaining the Gospel, I asked Luis if he would like to invite Jesus into his life. His answer was, "Si." So under the shady tree in that remote jungle setting, Luis asked Jesus to be his Savior.

As we continued our afternoon walk, I explained some basics to help him grow as a new believer. Once we arrived at the airstrip, Luis enthusiastically shared his newfound faith with his companions. Our construction crew celebrated Luis's conversion, and I gave him a Spanish New Testament that I carried in the plane.

We came into the jungle to hunt for game, but God had something much bigger on the agenda. We walked away with an eternal prize. I'll never forget the beautiful smile on Luis's face as he came to the Lord. He looked at me and said, "*Capitán, estoy muy contento*," or, in English, "I am very happy."

Luis, hunting guide, who received Christ during hunting trip

Banana trees, flying ants, and a new member in "The Family"

1964-1969

When I opened an airstrip near the Cubeo village in southeastern Colombia, it was like so many other jungle airstrips—tricky, but marginally safe. When I returned a few months later, rapidly growing banana trees at the end of the runway stood twenty feet high. I needed to clip the tops of the trees just to get my plane on the ground.

The banana trees had to go!

But as Jay Salser, the Bible translator for these Cubeo-speaking people interpreted my remarks into the local language of the gathered crowd, I could see that this wasn't going to be an easy sell. Using Jay as his interpreter, Capitán Pedro, the village chief, informed me, "We don't want to cut them down. Each tree represents a stalk of cooking or eating bananas, a staple of the Cubeos."

After further conversation and negotiation, we reached a compromise. Since each stalk was valued at five pesos, I paid the owners fifty pesos (about $2.00), and they agreed to remove ten trees. Done!

I unloaded the Salsers' food, mail, medicines, and a fresh battery for the short-wave radio, enough to keep them supplied for a few more weeks in the village. By then, the banana trees had been removed, and I had room to take off and head to my next jungle destination.

Some months later, I arrived with three visitors from the United States. They were interested in meeting the Cubeo people and the Salser family. We arrived late in the afternoon, crossed the river in a dugout canoe, and spent the night in the village.

As we visited with Jay, and his wife, Neva, in their mud house with palm leaf roof, a man suddenly burst into the open doorway, talking loudly in Cubeo. Jay listened, then clued us in on the topic—flying ants. A light rain, the first after a long dry season, had fallen on ant holes in the ground. The raindrops triggered the hatching of thousands of flying ants. Clouds of the tiny creatures filled the air. The whole village turned out to harvest the delicacy. The people—men, women, and children, all filled their baskets by the handful as we watched. Quickly eating a handful of live ants, a man approached one of the visitors, offering another handful.

I smiled as I watched the reaction. No way were the visitors interested in partaking. Then it was my turn. I took the offering and popped the ants into my mouth, legs, wings, and all. I could feel them moving as I began chewing. The taste was strange but a little like bacon, very little!

Lord, I'll eat them up if you keep them down, was an appropriate prayer in this situation. I did manage to keep them down, except for the legs and wings that caught between my teeth. (I wondered if the Cubeos knew about toothbrushes.)

Then I noticed an open fire nearby with a large clay griddle heating for the feast. Tossing a large quantity of the crawling creatures onto the makeshift frying pan, a woman began stirring with a stick. Slowly, the mass of creatures stopped moving as the ants succumbed to the cooking process.

Now, let's see how they taste. Much better, thank you!

Forrest Zander

Cooking flour on clay griddle over open fire—griddle also served to cook the flying ants

1972-77

Some years later, I visited the same village as Field Director in Colombia. We landed on the same airstrip, now considerably longer and safer. We crossed the same river in a dugout canoe, and I greeted many of the same people. As I checked on the well-being of the missionary translators, I noticed someone was missing.

Where was Capitán Pedro?

Jay explained that Capitán Pedro, now quite elderly, was sick and not able to get around very well. "Would you like to visit him?" Jay asked.

Of course!

His Faithfulness Reaches to the Skies

We walked to the chief's house a short distance away. As we entered and greeted the sick man, he sat up in his hammock and smiled. He seemed pleased to see me and called me by name. For a few minutes we exchanged pleasantries, with Jay interpreting. I mentioned key events in our relationship, including how he led his villagers in the construction of the airstrip that allowed me to make my first flight to their village. I talked about the friendship we had enjoyed over the years. Then the Holy Spirit quickened my heart and urged me to share my faith with the old chief. With Jay assuring me that this was okay, I again mentioned our friendship and said that there was just one aspect that was lacking.

"We are not brothers spiritually, and I wish we were," I said.

When the chief responded, Jay got visibly excited.

"This is important," Jay said, "Pedro says he wants to 'learn more.' In the Cubeo culture, this means he wants to learn all that your wish entails, and then he will commit himself to that new knowledge. In a sense he is making a pre-commitment to Christ."

Wow!

Over the next six months, Jay spent time teaching Pedro from the Scriptures he had translated. He explained exactly what a commitment to the Lord is all about. Then one day we received a radio message from Jay. "Today, Capitán Pedro has joined 'The Family.'"

There was no question about what he meant. Our hearts rejoiced. Another lost soul found his way home through the

Word of God in his mother tongue.

Forrest with Cubeo Chief, Capitán Pedro, who came to faith after I had shared my faith with him

A badly burned baby

1966

While on the mission field, we faced difficult, sometimes heartbreaking challenges. One such experience occurred when the baby daughter of one of our center employees was victim of a fire that destroyed their palm leaf roofed house. To protect the baby from the leaky roof, a sheet of plastic covered her bed like a tiny tent. However, as the fire spread, the plastic caught fire and dripped melting plastic on the poor baby's body. Before anyone could save her, she was badly burned. She also breathed the acrid smoke, causing further medical complications. The nurse brought the baby to the hangar, in a tub of ice water, hoping to alleviate the extensive burns.

Decision time!

The only hope for this baby girl was treatment at the children's hospital in Bogotá—a hundred miles away. The flight over the Andes Mountains required crossing a rugged ridge about 11,000 feet in elevation. It was often cloud-covered, in which case the flight would be on instruments with the minimum entry altitude at 15,000 feet. Furthermore, it was late afternoon, and sunset would soon be upon us. Here was the problem: At the time our single-engine aircraft were not allowed to fly an instrument flight plan nor fly at night. Flight regulations required that we be on the ground fifteen minutes before sunset, which was always around 6 PM.

The nurse gathered her things, and I grabbed my overnight bag. This was going to be close. Departing after 5 PM required that I declare an emergency, which allowed for some deviation from flight rules. Climbing to 11,000 feet, we approached the mountains to take a look.

The ridge was clear of clouds!

I contacted the control tower and explained the emergency, requesting priority landing and an ambulance. Entering the Bogotá valley, I could see the beautiful city now immersed in thousands of lights, and the airport runway lights. The landing was uneventful, and we taxied to the ramp where the ambulance waited.

After securing the aircraft, I jumped in the ambulance with the crew, nurse, and water tub with baby. Little did I realize that we were in for the ride of our lives. Entering rush hour traffic, the driver threw all caution to the wind and drove like a maniac. When he came to a stoplight and traffic didn't get out of the way, with lights flashing and siren blaring, he drove onto the sidewalk to get through the intersections. I couldn't believe this was happening. Pedestrians beware, here we come, ready or not.

We arrived at the children's hospital in record time, all the way across this city of 8 million people. Turning the baby over to the emergency staff, I exited with my head swimming.

The nurse stayed with the baby. We hoped and prayed for the best. But a few days later we received the sad news that the baby had succumbed to her injuries and died.

These heart-wrenching experiences are never easy, but I believe God has a bigger plan, and Jesus will one day wipe away every tear from our eyes.

One of the joys of missionary flying was to be on duty for these medical emergencies, to be in a position to save a life that otherwise might perish due to lack of proper medicine or distance from a hospital. Giving up part of Christmas Day or another holiday with family to make an emergency trip was part of the job.

An Indian wedding

1967

Etelvina, a young Tucano woman, had come to Lomalinda to

help Betty and Birdie, a team of single women, translate the Scriptures in the Tucano language. Meanwhile, Emiliano, a young man from a neighboring language group, the Piratapuyo, was working in Lomalinda, learning carpentry skills and building homes for the missionaries.

Boy meets girl, and wedding bells begin to ring. But marriage in Colombia is not easy. Bride and groom must appear before a judge and be married in a civil ceremony with appropriate sponsors. That's how Margaret and I got involved.

I flew the couple to the state capital and served as "best man" and sponsor. Betty and Birdie were "bridesmaids" and sponsors. The ceremony took place in the judge's chambers where papers were signed and the marriage became legal and official. By afternoon we were on our way home.

Meanwhile, Margaret was preparing food and decorating our living room for the wedding reception. Over 100 guests—missionaries, language helpers, and assorted people, welcomed the new bride and groom home.

Margaret wrote, "The reception was complete with punch (and bowl), lovely cake, lace tablecloth, organ music (folding organ), nervous groom, and nonchalant bride. I made her dress!" We had a great time, took lots of photos, and almost felt like parents to this new couple.

Emiliano and Etelvina established their home nearby and continued to work with us at the center. And Betty and Birdie eventually translated the entire New Testament in the Tucano language.

Forrest Zander

Tranquil jungle scene at Acaricuara on the Papurí River, southeastern Colombia, Betty and Birdie's tribal location and home of bride, Etelvina

Anita's mysterious illness and recovery

1967

Margaret's notes from our 1967 annual letter:

July: After three weeks of illness, we take Anita to a doctor in Bogotá.

August: Anita has extensive tests, but the source of her illness is as yet undiagnosed. Daddy visits us every two weeks. Anita has a heart murmur which miraculously disappears. Anita loses her very first tooth and is growing very rapidly in spite of her illness.

His Faithfulness Reaches to the Skies

September: Anita does not improve and no diagnosis is made; therefore, according to the book of James, we call in the "elders" to have a special prayer for her. Acting upon the Lord's promises, we return to the Lomalinda Center. Anita begins Kindergarten.

October: We 'farm out' our daughters (Anita here and Arlene in Bogotá) and go on a flying survey to western Colombia.

November: Anita sports her first fillings. Both girls are in perfect health according to their doctor.

December: Arlene celebrates her second Christmas by using her sixteen teeth to bite a ***glass*** ornament into a jillion pieces. We got all the glass from her mouth with only one small cut. How could anything so pretty not be good to eat?

Baby Anita enjoying her first Christmas in the U.S. at Grandma Morgan's in Oregon

Anita playing in the snow at Grandma's

Flying safely

1968

One of my important responsibilities as Chief Pilot in Colombia was to establish rules and regulations that conformed to norms established by the Colombian Civil Aviation authorities. In addition, there were internal rules that governed how and where we would fly in the jungles, which required greater safety margins. In those days GPS was unknown, so the known location of the aircraft at all times was extremely important. Air routes were established to distant jungle destinations with checkpoints along the way. Pilots were required to radio their position, time, and altitude every 15 to 20 minutes to our flight following service. These were carefully noted in a log at our operational center by trained radio operators. We had a special provision from the government to operate single engine aircraft in the jungles. In case of engine failure, the need to pinpoint location for search and rescue operations was critical.

I established minimum altitudes for flying in bad weather. All of these details were taught to new pilots during a period of check flights before they were allowed to fly solo. I logged many hours in the right seat teaching the norms, and observing how closely the new pilot followed them. Because many of our jungle airstrips were of minimal length and width due to the difficulty of removing large trees, every new pilot had to demonstrate his ability to land and take off safely from each airstrip.

Another challenge involved navigating in the jungles where checkpoints were minimal, and inclement weather could restrict visibility and recognition. Crossovers from one river system to another required leaving one river at a designated checkpoint and flying a compass heading for some time over dense jungle, hoping to intersect the next river at a known point.

Some crossovers could be as long as one hour without a safe place to land in case of engine trouble. If a problem occurred, the radio operator (in Peru) would sound "a general" on the center party line phone system. Six long rings would alert everyone near a phone on the center to pray for the safety of the pilot and passengers.

In Peru, during a long crossover, the pilot in a float plane encountered an engine failure near its mid-point at an altitude of several thousand feet. His only recourse was to glide to a small stream hardly wider than the plane's wingspan. He expertly guided it between the tree-lined banks, touched down in a portion of the stream with several inches of water and came to a stop on a tiny beach. The pilot and passenger were unhurt, and the plane undamaged. The problem was how to extricate the plane from this difficult location.

The Lord's intervention in this situation was obvious. Located near the stream was a school with a soccer field of sufficient length to allow a wheel plane to land with a replacement engine and some mechanics. Somehow they were able to remove the damaged engine and fly it out for repair in the wheel plane. The new engine was installed in the float plane, and during high water, with just a pilot to minimize its weight, the plane was extricated from the small stream and flown back to the mission center.

His Faithfulness Reaches to the Skies

Forrest organized and managed the new aviation program in Colombia. Forrest with Helio Courier aircraft in which he logged hundreds of flight hours

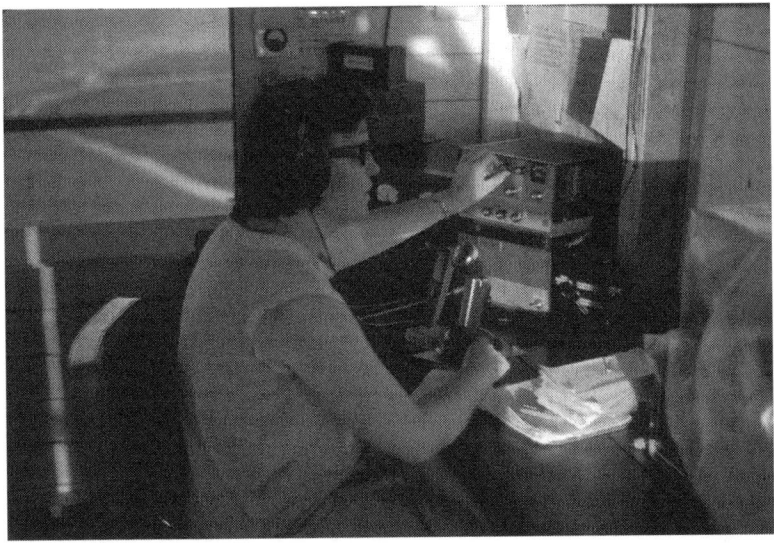

Margaret on shortwave radio following flights over the jungle

Crossing the cultural divide

Margaret writes, "Dry season brought winds of some 35 mph from morning to evening. Roads turned to powdered dust that blew into homes. During construction of a nearby bridge, trucks hauling materials stirred up the dust. Children in the nearby town who lived in homes beside the roads became ill with dust pneumonia or from contaminated water. Four children died in one day. One father asked us what they could do to stem the tide. When Forrey mentioned that boiling the water would stave off some illnesses, the father replied that the boiling of water wasn't their custom."

His Faithfulness Reaches to the Skies

More heroes and Christmas 1968

1968

Ron Metzger arrived in Colombia as a single missionary, trained in linguistics. He was eager to begin working with a people group who needed to know Jesus, who spoke a language that had no alphabet and no described grammatical system, and who would be open to Ron living among them and eventually translating God's Word for them. Having no place to live at our mission center, Ron was invited to occupy our guest room and be part of our family in his early days on the field.

God led Ron to the Carapana people, a small tribe, virtually forgotten, of just a few hundred souls. Scattered in the eastern jungles of Colombia, on a small tributary of the Vaupes River, they lived as hunters and fishermen, supplemented by slash and burn agriculture.

To reach the Carapana, Ron needed to take an arduous journey consisting of a two-and-a-half hour flight to a rubber gatherer's jungle ranch, followed by a one hour trip in a motorized canoe down the Vaupes to a huge waterfall. There a gigantic rock formation created a beautiful but dangerous obstacle, forcing the entire river to spill over the rock dam. (Apparently a number of travelers lost their lives trying to get past the falls. The falls were called *Yurupari*—the falls of the devil.) A portage around the falls with baggage took an additional hour by land. Then, hopefully, another motorized canoe would be available for hire to convey him down a further stretch of the main river. That leg of the journey consumed the rest of the first day. As nightfall approached, it was necessary to find a campsite or abandoned house in which to spend the night. The trip continued into the second day on the main river. Finally, the canoe arrived at the confluence of a smaller tributary, called Cano Ti, where it emptied into the main river. The primary Carapana village where Ron would settle was still another two hours up this narrow, log-filled tributary. The entire river trip would take about two days.

Margaret and I offered to help. We would travel with Ron on this dangerous trip to the village and assist the Carapana people in building an airstrip. The completed airstrip would reduce the 2-day trip by river to a seventeen minute flight. We decided to go, taking Anita (6) and Arlene (18 months) with us. We would be in the village for over two weeks.

Due to bad weather, we got a late start and arrived at the rubber gatherer's ranch in late afternoon. It was too late for the pilot to return, so he spent the night with us. During the night Arlene woke us with a fever. Now we were faced with a decision: *Do we go on with the trip or return Margaret and the girls back home on the plane?* Once again Margaret showed spiritual insight; she decided that this was an attack of the enemy. We agreed that we would proceed and trust the Lord for a good outcome.

We endured the canoe trips and the portage around the falls, spending the night in an abandoned jungle house. Hurrying to set up camp before darkness fell, we strung two hammocks for the girls to sleep in. Then Margaret and I placed a mosquito net over each of the girls and slept on the floor beneath them. Not having any cooking facilities in this primitive place, our supper and breakfast consisted of a few bags of corn curls and water from our canteens.

His Faithfulness Reaches to the Skies

Arriving in the village, hot and tired, but safe and sound, Arlene showed us the cause of the fever. She was cutting her two-year molars at 18 months. Ron and I joined the villagers in working on the airstrip while Margaret prepared the meals for Ron and me. The village men and women joined in, clearing the trees, brush, and roots. Huge stumps slowed the work but we could see progress each day. The cleared area was nearly 150 meters, enough for an emergency flight if necessary.

The bad news came the next morning over the shortwave radio. Ron's mother in Maryland had died unexpectedly as a result of heart surgery. We were all shocked and saddened at this unanticipated news. Ron was about to depart by river to travel to be with his family. I told Ron that we should call for the plane, three hours away. If we could remove the large stump at the end of the cleared area, the plane could land. The villagers and we worked diligently. Ten minutes before the plane's arrival, the stump was finally removed and the huge hole filled in! Whew!

Ron was evacuated, and within 48 hours he was with his family in Maryland. We stayed another ten days and saw the airstrip extended to operational length. After that, we were able to enjoy the seventeen minute flight over the rivers and waterfalls to the rubber gatherer's ranch. Then another 2.5 hours and we were home at the Lomalinda Center.

Later in the year, as Christmas approached, we decided to vacation at Ron's village and enjoy the holiday there. I went hunting with some of the Carapana men on Christmas Eve to a water hole deep in the jungle where they said a tapir (jungle cow) would probably be enjoying a cool bath. Sure enough, there he was as we snuck up to the site. The 300 lb. tapir took off at full speed, running right across our path. One man shot first and missed. I was next and nailed him in a vital spot. He crashed into the brush where we were able to secure him for the night. As nightfall approached, we hurried to the village to find our way back before dark. Christmas Day we made our way to the tapir, butchered him, and cut him into pieces. Most of the villagers were there to carry their portion of the meat, and everyone feasted on the Christmas dinner the Lord had provided for us.

Sometime later, Ron and Lois, a new missionary, became friends. Love blossomed, and Ron acquired a wife and ministry partner. They persevered for 25 years in the village, and with a team of men translated the entire New Testament into Carapana. They saw the Word transform the lives of our Carapana friends. Over their years of dedicated service, we were their "prayer partners," praying regularly for them.

The Carapana planned a dedication of the New Testament in their jungle village. Ron and Lois invited us to be there. We flew out with several guests, landing on a now extended and adequate airstrip, much improved from our earlier time. We gathered in the "maloca," a large communal palm leaf dwelling where several families lived. Each family had its own space, almost like a motel. A large open area served well for the dedication service. A Carapana girl entered and walked up the center aisle, with a candle, indicating the arrival of the light of the Word of God. Next, another entered with an open New Testament itself. Music in their language was part of the service, accompanied by Carapana men on guitars. Ron asked me to give the dedicatory prayer in Spanish, which he interpreted in the Carapana language. Then a big surprise! Margaret and I were given a gold bound Carapana New Testament, with an expression of gratitude in Spanish for our years of encouragement and prayer partnership in this work, written on the flyleaf. The team of five Carapana co-translators, men who had assisted Ron and Lois at various times during those years of labor, were each presented with their copy of the New Testament. Everyone then joined in the fiesta with abundant local Carapana food.

Maloca, typical communal house, occupied by clan (extended family). Each family had its own closed area inside like a motel. In the rear was an open area for gathering in the evenings, and the cooking area was sometimes attached to the main maloca.

Completing this phase of their calling, Ron and Lois later moved to the Colombian islands of San Andres and Providencia in the Caribbean. There they trained and encouraged a team of Christians to translate the New Testament into Islander Creole, the indigenous island language. Though Lois was later called Home, Ron has continued this project and will soon see the Islander Creole New Testament in print. It will also be available in audio format for use in Islander schools and radio programs. Ron and Lois are among my spiritual heroes, providing mother tongue Scriptures for two more Colombian languages.

The Paez people

One of the joys of being Field Director was visiting translators in their villages in the jungles and mountains of Colombia. I had heard about Marianna Slocum and Florence Gerdel and their work of translating the New Testament into both highland and lowland Tzeltal languages in southern Mexico. There was a great turning to the Lord, and they entrusted the continuing ministry to local Tzeltal believers. Having completed all this, they traveled to Colombia to begin translation work in a third language in their lifetimes, a very unusual and exemplary investment of their lives. They became two more of the heroes of the faith with whom we worked in Colombia.

Our family had the great privilege of traveling to the mountains of central Colombia where Marianna and Florence spent many years translating the New Testament for the Paez people. The Lord had brought a number of Paez people to faith through the work of Christian & Missionary Alliance missionaries using the Spanish Scriptures. But the Paez believers hungered for a deeper understanding of God's will for them as Christians. One believer told me his story as we visited at his home outside of the town where he lived with his wife and children.

"Our hunger for understanding caused us to begin praying for Scriptures in our own Paez language. One day I was in our local town and was introduced to these two ladies, Marianna and Florence. They told me they had come to translate the New Testament into Paez. When I heard this news, I rejoiced that God was answering our prayers," he said. Many years passed as the ladies learned this difficult language, created an alphabet, analyzed the grammatical system, and prepared primers to help readers become fluent in Paez. The New Testament translation was completed and published for the Paez.

During our visit, Marianna and Florence told us about a weekend Bible conference in a remote area where Paez would gather to worship and hear the Word of God. They invited me to accompany them to visit the conference. We drove to the end of the road and then continued on horseback for two hours until we reached the chapel, site of the Bible conference. I was impressed as I experienced the conference led by Paez pastors and laymen, heard them singing worship songs in Paez, led by Paez musicians playing on guitars and other instruments. Then the Word in Paez was taught by various pastors as the conference continued during the weekend. This truly indigenous movement impressed me with the value of God's Word in Paez, their mother tongue.

Forrest Zander

Paez pastor in Andes highlands told me that, though they were Christians, reading the Scriptures in Spanish made them weep because they could not understand them.

Treated by a witch doctor

1970

Capitán Mario, village chief and medicine man, was seated before me observing the red-blue lines up my leg. The fungus infection in my foot was getting worse. Now I had blood poisoning, fever, and I was feeling awful. Mario began blowing on my leg, with his fingers gently moving down my leg, in an apparent attempt to take the infection back to its origin.

How did I get into this? Why is Mario treating me?

As missionaries, we experienced many situations where there simply wasn't an instruction manual. We had to use our best judgment. I was in a southern Barasano village in eastern

His Faithfulness Reaches to the Skies

Colombia, not far from the Brazilian border. As Field Director, I had the joy of visiting our translator teams in their ministry locations, hoping to better understand their needs so I could encourage and help them. But this infection wasn't part of the plan. I felt fine when I left our center of operations. By the time our flight arrived at this village three hours later, I was feeling sick and achy. My foot started to hurt, so I took off my sock and rolled up my pant leg. Sure enough—there were the signs of blood poisoning.

The translator's wife served as interpreter. Wanting to do this in the right way, I had asked her permission to witness to Mario, and she had agreed to translate from my Spanish to Mario's language. As he treated me, I reviewed our friendship over the years. This approach had worked well with another village chief who had responded to the gospel message. Mario and I reminisced about the first time our survey team had contacted the village. Mario, village chief at that time also, only knew two Spanish words, "Americano" and "Medico" (doctor). He asked two questions using those words. Would the people coming to live in his village be Americans? *Yes.* And would they be doctors? (*Well, yes, they would have medicines for snake bite and malaria.*) So Mario consented to our translator team coming to live in his village.

Fortunately for me, the translator team also had penicillin on hand—the indicated treatment for blood poisoning. They provided me with an injection almost as soon as I arrived in the village.

So as Mario attempted to treat me in his customary way, I didn't resist. If I had, I would probably have offended him and turned him off to the witness I was trying to convey. As it was, the penicillin had its proper effect, and soon I was my old self again. And Mario remained my friend.

Jungle chief and Shaman (often referred to as Witch Doctor) learning to read and write his mother tongue for the first time

The fire

1971

It was a peaceful Sunday afternoon at the height of the dry season. The kids were napping or playing quietly. Margaret was away for the weekend with a friend in the capital town of our state. I heard in the distance what sounded like small explosions. A prairie grass fire, fed by 35 mph winds, had progressed to the edge of our Lomalinda Center. Smoke was everywhere. The sounds were the concrete-asbestos sheets of roofing popping from the extreme heat as the home of the Morgan family was on fire. They lost everything in their home except the refrigerator which Frank Morgan was able to extricate at the last minute. Other homes were in danger. Backfires were quickly set to stop the advancing flames. I quickly got the kids up and took them to a safe area, dropping them off at the communal dining room. Other wives were there with their kids as the men rushed off to fight the fire. I joined the bucket brigade. The Lord's presence was with all of us in a wonderful way. Only one house was destroyed and no lives were lost. That Sunday evening, at our usual time to hear reports from translators recently returned from their villages, we spent time praising the Lord for His mercy and grace. We also learned we needed to be better prepared the next dry season. Backfires were routinely set before any were needed. A donated fire truck became an essential part of the preparation to keep backfires under control. All center personnel became acutely aware of the dangers; no fires were set unless they were necessary, and all fires were attended at all times.

Growing up in Colombia:

My children share their memories

Alby

I remember…

…the prairie grass fires being pretty scary.

…my epic fail wipe out in front of everyone at Wheelers when

I thought I had learned to ride a bike. I hit the fence and every picket on it.

..."sledding" down the bamboo leaf hill on a piece of cardboard.

...swimming and having the baby pirahna nibble on us and not really being phased by it. Then when swimming in Uncle Lowell's water hole in Illinois, we would freak out when the sun fish would nibble on us.

When you were gone, we loved Mom making oatmeal and brown sugar, and her reading *Little House on the Prairie*—the whole series.

Arlene

I still have a ginormous scar on my leg from wiping out in a sand pit in front of Wheelers. It was so huge it took months to heal.

The bamboo leaf hill sledding was hot and itchy! That little black fur on the bamboo leaves would coat us and itch. But it was still very fun. I remember us coaxing Benjamin Lopez (a visiting government official) to do it. He just filmed us for a while, and we finally convinced him to try it.

The nibbling piranhas were great at taking care of the two warts on my right knee for me. I tended to scrape them, and they would bleed which REALLY attracted the piranhas!

The scariest thing for me was always the prairie fires. The smell of burning grass can still make me tear up, and I have to stamp down the terror. There is a great picture on the Lomalinda Facebook page of a fire at night. Most of our friends say that they associate the smell of burning grass with Christmas (dry season). One time I woke up from a Sunday afternoon nap to the snapping sound of sheets on the line blowing in the wind. I looked out the window, and there were no sheets on the line! Then the sound registered with the smell of smoke—the jungle was on fire and the snapping was the crackle of the fire.

We walked up the hill toward the center of the community, eventually passing about 20 houses but...still no people. It was the most quiet and deserted I had ever seen it, and the only sound was the cracking and roaring of the fire. Usually there were birds tweeting and monkeys howling and parrots calling and lots of natural noises. But this time, silence and the roar of fire. We finally reached the dining hall where we found several moms and kids gathered. Some were already crying over the loss of their homes and the imminent loss of others. It seemed to me that the fire wasn't going to stop until we were all consumed. And we were worried about the men out fighting it with nothing but buckets.

Then there was the emergency landing, and then the next one and then the landslide. Oh, and the bombing. And Alby saying that he never knew if Dad would come home alive at night.

And that doesn't even take into account the fun stuff! Chi-chi the monkey hitching a ride from room to room on our legs; Pepe the parrot and some of his ilk deliberately playing tricks on me and screaming just to scare me; playing Old Maid as a family in the hammock, seeing how high we could swing in it or climb up it before it dumped us onto the floor. May was mango month, and we ate them till they were coming out of our ears; then Mom made jelly from them. Putting the big kettle on to boil our (lake) water at night so that we had enough purified water to drink. Finding worms, ants, and roaches in EVERYTHING. Roaches running over my legs at night between the sheets. Dad locking us in the bathroom and chasing the bats around the house with the shotgun. (Note: It was a .22 rifle.) The loud echoing of the lizards running thru the attic at night. Going down to get a glass of water in the early morning and finding a dinosaur (7-foot iguana) in the kitchen. I broke the sound barrier running back upstairs. (See, we really did have monsters under our beds.) The snake who strangled himself trying to climb into my room between the studs in the wall. Field Day. County Fair where my 2 layer chocolate cake won first prize—as a second grader! The military invasion. Katherine and I were playing right where they landed the helicopters, and I was sure I was going to get shot on the spot! Learning to ride a bike on a gravel/sand road. Camping in the jungle. The "help-me" frogs calling at night. How scary it was that Mom and Dad would leave us with a sitter and go gator hunting at night.

Surviving a near crash landing

1972-1977

During takeoff from the International Airport, Bogotá, Colombia, in a chartered DC-3, the left engine malfunctioned just after lift-off. At an elevation of 8,350 feet above sea level, this particular plane barely climbs with one engine at full power. The pilot declared an emergency, was cleared to land, and just managed to put the aircraft back on the runway. Twenty-three of us missionaries were on board, including our children and several others. We sighed with relief as we disembarked.

For the next half hour, mechanics worked on the engine. Then the pilot announced a successful repair, and called for us to reboard. In my mind, the repair needed to be verified. So I spoke with the pilot, asking him to test fly the aircraft without passengers to make sure the repair was successful. But he was adamant that the DC-3 was okay. One mother with three children was so upset that she and her children left to wait for another day. The remaining nineteen of us boarded. Again we taxied out to the active runway. Again we were cleared for take-off, and roared into the sky, only to hear the same engine malfunction, this time closer to the ground.

Only a miracle would get us safely back on the ground this time.

Not knowing of our predicament, my parents in Illinois were extremely burdened for our safety and stopped to pray. Somehow—probably with the assistance of a few angels—the pilot made the necessary turns to position us for landing. I looked down and saw a house so close that I felt like I could almost touch it. Everyone on board was praying for a safe landing. I could see the runway, but the plane still needed to make a 90-degree left turn to get into its final approach. We were so low that it looked impossible. We began the turn very, very low, and then rolled out of it just as the tires screeched to announce our touchdown.

Whew! Thank you, Lord!

As Field Director of our work in Colombia and an experienced pilot, I didn't want any of our missionaries to experience a similar situation in the future. I declared the airline unfit for our business. We made alternative arrangements to get to Lomalinda—a three-hour road trip over rugged mountains, followed by another six-hour ride on a dusty bus. We made it back home, exhausted, but safe.

Typical service to rural areas in Colombia. Fare is the same inside, outside, or on top.

What happened to Ron

Earlier I shared the first part of the story, "Flying with danger." Ron was scheduled to fly to an "impossible" airstrip in the mountains of Colombia to drop off missionaries and cargo. I expected him back well before ten o'clock in the morning. But the hours rolled by with no sign of our missing pilot, and no way to reach him by radio. All I could imagine was burning wreckage in the side of a mountain with Ron inside.

Finally, at four o'clock in the afternoon, I heard the drone of an airplane. And sure enough, in flew Ron.

When he got out of the airplane, Ron's face was as long as I've ever seen. He said to me, "You can't guess what happened. I landed safely, taxied to the top end of the airstrip, set the parking brake, and started to unload. The parking brake didn't hold, and the plane rolled backwards down the other side of the airstrip into a fence. The rudder was badly bent. It took all day to make a temporary repair. Take a look."

He was right. The tail was badly bent. His first damage to an aircraft in his flying career. But the real damage was to Ron's spirit. Professional pilots take great pride in their ability to operate safely and to avoid accidents. This one had nothing to do with his ability or professionalism. But the tail was bent.

I removed my chief pilot's hat at that moment. I put on my chaplain's hat. I turned to 1 Samuel chapter 30 and read the first six verses to Ron. In this passage, things weren't going David's way. His village had been attacked while he and his men were away. The women and children had been carried off in the raid. And now his men were talking about stoning him to death. But David found strength or encouraged himself in the Lord his God. I read that to Ron, and said, "I want to encourage you in the Lord."

I later became Field Director of Wycliffe's work in Colombia, and found that one of my main responsibilities was to encourage my fellow missionaries. And Ron—he went on to become one of Wycliffe's best pilots in Colombia.

Most difficult airstrip (light upper area) gives illusion of flatness but is really a steep upslope. Airstrip where Ron had to deal with a damaged tail that took all day to repair

Chapter 5

DIPLOMACY

Missionaries in jail

1966

Sometime in 1966, early in the history of our center of operations, a colonel appeared at our door. He introduced himself as the Commander of the Army Artillery School in Bogotá. When he saw my pregnant wife in this remote place so far from a hospital, he expressed his concern, maybe envisioning his wife in a similar situation. Then he told us he had come with his troops and officers-in-training, and they were setting up an artillery range in an uninhabited area not far away. They would be shooting Howitzers and other cannons and would be making a lot of noise. It was kind of him to warn us of the impending disturbance.

Later he returned and asked a favor, "My officers need to see the range from the air. Would you fly them in your plane and do figure eights over the guns and the targets? Using smoke shells, they can observe if they are on target and radio their corrections to the ground." I was happy to comply as I had heard about this type of aerial observation and thought it would be fun to do, at the same time being helpful to them.

The commander was happy and even paid for the flights.

During their field operations, Margaret and I invited him and the trainee officers to our home and we enjoyed dinner together. The colonel stopped by to say farewell after completing their mission. During that visit, he gave us his phone number and asked us to look him up the next time we were in Bogotá. Then he departed with his convoy of military trucks, jeeps, and mobile cannons.

Later, Margaret and I enjoyed dinner in his home with some of the officers we had met, this time with their wives. And when our daughter Arlene was born (August 3, 1966), he sent a lovely floral piece to honor her arrival.

1974-1979

Over the ensuing years, we lost contact with the colonel.

But then one day I received a desperate phone call from our missionary pilot and linguist in northern Colombia. The Colombian army had mistaken them for drug runners and had them under arrest. They were allowed one phone call. I had 48 hours to secure their release, or they would face a minimum mandatory sentence of six months in a Colombian jail.

How did this happen?

A new Helio Courier aircraft had recently arrived in the country, and we were in the process of transferring the registration from U.S. to Colombian. We hadn't planned to use it until the new numbers were painted on the fuselage and wings. But one of the fleet was in maintenance and unavailable to make a flight to the far north, so we sent our U.S. registered aircraft instead. What we didn't know is that U.S. registered aircraft in this region were making illegal flights to pick up "Colombian Gold"—marijuana destined for markets in the southern U.S. One successful flight could make a pilot rich, and 90% of those flights managed to evade detection.

Helio Courier on jungle airstrip

What to do?

As Field Director, the weight of their safety was on my shoulders. I went to the Ministerio de Defensa, the Colombian equivalent of the Pentagon, a huge complex just outside the city. Since they were held by the Army, I went to that division. But with dozens of offices, one for every department in the Army, where would I begin? I decided to start at the top. Entering the commander's office, I gave the receptionist my business card and asked to see the general. I waited, wondering if a foreign stranger without an appointment would even be considered. Suddenly, the general burst out of his office, greeted me with the traditional "abrazo" (bear-hug), and called me by name.

It took me a moment, and then I realized: here was the former Commander of the Artillery!

He invited me into his impressive office, and we spent a few minutes reminiscing. Then we finally got to the purpose of my visit. As I explained the plight of our two missionaries in jail, he nodded understandingly. Then he reached for a red telephone on his desk, a "hot" line directly to the commander in the drug area. The general spoke into the receiver, "Guess who's in my office today? Remember Capitán Zander? He flew you officers so smoothly on those maneuvers that none of you got airsick."

Here the commander of the drug area was one of the officers-in-training I had flown in my plane years earlier.

The general set down the phone and told me the men would be freed immediately.

Only the Lord could have orchestrated these events, weaving them together over years of time, and using friendships forged in service to the Army to work a miracle of gigantic proportions. Even after all these years, I am still in awe at the grace and kindness of the Lord in caring for His people and His mission.

His Faithfulness Reaches to the Skies

Standing before the president

1964-1969

When I first visited Moody Bible Institute in 1950 or 1951, Ralph Snow, Dean of Men, said to me, "Forrest, if you become a missionary pilot, you may stand before presidents and kings and represent the Lord."

As I shared above, I had opportunity to meet the president of Ecuador early in my career. A few years later, I met the president of Colombia. Here's how it happened:

Colombian officials called me and asked if they could borrow a Wycliffe airplane and my services as pilot. They needed to get the president of the country from an airstrip where his plane could land, out to a remote jungle area in the middle of the rainy season, when the roads were impassable. So I had the privilege of meeting the president, flying him and several of his ministers into this remote area.

1972

Later, when I became the director of Wycliffe's work in Colombia and our mission organization was celebrating its 10th anniversary, one of my friends in the government said, "You people have been here for ten years. The president needs to express appreciation for your work."

He arranged an interview with the president for me and my assistant. He took us to the executive office in the Presidential Palace, and there the president expressed appreciation for

Wycliffe's work. I returned and conveyed his appreciation to all the Wycliffe missionaries.

The bomb

1974

Arriving from the Bogotá International Airport with a new family, my assistant, Bill Nyman, was dropping them off at our guest house. One of the guests, first at the door, noticed a package and picked it up. Bill recognized it immediately and yelled, "It's a bomb." The guest immediately dropped it, and all of them ducked behind the car just as the bomb exploded at the door. No one was injured, but the powerful blast broke the windows in the guest house and every other house within a half block.

I quickly drove over to be with our missionaries and to inspect the damage. The metal door was turned into shrapnel that went flying throughout the first floor. We found a piece the size of my fist, which had passed through a door and was embedded in the wall at the extreme back of the house. Another piece of shrapnel about the same size had blown through the door of a storage area, completely severed a two by four, and became embedded in a suitcase. There was broken glass all over. Fortunately, all the occupants were asleep in upper floors, and all lives were safe, with only a few minor cuts from flying glass. The Lord's mercy was obvious. We were aware that our enemies wanted our mission out of the country, but we didn't know they would resort to such deadly tactics.

"You must leave the country!"[4]

1971-1979

"You have one year to get out of our country."

The Colombian official wasn't joking. As an emissary for the president, he had the full authority to tell us to leave. We were being evicted. Our mission was being kicked out of Colombia.

The full impact of his words began to settle in. Decades of work washed away. Years of prayer and negotiation to win the right to enter the country. Thousands of hours of hacking through jungles, building airstrips, learning languages, building relationships, repairing airplanes, teaching agriculture, translating Scripture, and beginning to share the Gospel. Years of preparation by hundreds of people, now on the threshold of bearing fruit—all potentially washed away.

"I speak for the president. Your mission must leave Colombia." The official brought me back from my thoughts.

I couldn't blame the president. The pressure was getting to him. His officials were constantly harassed by our opponents who wanted to take over our linguistic and anthropological work.

"When are you going to kick the gringos out of the country?" they asked.

To add to the pressure, our enemies "leaked" misinformation (translation: lies) about us to the press. There was no telling what you might read about us in the newspaper. Rumor circu-

---

[4] Adapted from Shaw, Thomas and Clough, Dwight, *Amazing Faith* (Chicago: Moody Publishers), 2003. Used by permission of the authors.

lated that we were operating a uranium mine. Though it seemed ridiculous, people throughout Colombia were taking it seriously. People believed we had a hidden agenda. Instead of digging wells and teaching villagers how to get a better harvest, instead of learning cultures and languages, instead of operating a flying ambulance service, we were mining uranium from the lake at our center in Lomalinda. We were accused of flying uranium clandestinely at night to Washington, D.C. in our single engine airplanes, where it was made into who knows what! (Nuclear weapons maybe.) Another rumor held that our 15,000 gallon water storage tanks at the top of the hills at Lomalinda were not cisterns, but instead were missile silos!

How could anybody believe this? I wondered. But one of our friends pointed to the reporter who was printing some of these stories. "Take this journalist seriously," he said. "He has deposed ministers from the president's cabinet by writing about them. Now he's on your case." It became so bad, that I was afraid to pick up the papers in the morning, wondering what new lies would be invented about us.

The lead article in Colombia's most prestigious newspaper said it all. "The government finds its back to the wall and has no recourse but to cancel the contract with [our mission]," the article began. Day after day, attacks in the newspapers were escalating. Now the newly appointed Secretary General of the Government[5], Dr. Darío Vera Jimenez, to whom we reported, was being influenced by them. I immediately requested an appointment to attempt to foster his friendship. Walking into his office was like entering a cold storage unit. He had a cold, hard,

---

5Similar to the Secretary of the Interior but much more prestigious

unfriendly look on his face. After a curt greeting, he sat down, and I began to explain our work in the jungles and mountains with the ethnic languages. I had brought a sample of books in some of the languages created by our linguist-translators. The atmosphere warmed a bit and by the time I left, I was encouraged that he escorted me to the door, a very important gesture in his country.

Our family had recently moved to the capital, Bogotá, for just this reason: to develop relationships with key officials who had authority to keep us or dismiss us. This particular official carried considerable weight with the president.

Soon after this visit, I invited him to dinner in our apartment. The invitation was for 7 PM. Knowing that they are usually an hour late, Margaret planned to serve dinner at eight. By eight-thirty they were still no-shows. We decided they would be too embarrassed to be that late, so Margaret served dinner to three other guests and our family. About nine, just as we were finishing the delicious dinner, there was a knock on the door. Margaret was about to open the door when she viewed through the peek-hole an elegantly dressed woman. She made me answer the door. In a 1971 letter, Margaret described what followed: "I sent the girls to bed—they had eaten the guests' jello—and put on three more plates. One other factor was that there were three guests instead of two. Fortunately, as the Lord would have it, I had cooked an extra steak. We showed pictures and… they left at 11:30."

Margaret continued, "…we were rather relieved to see them go. Forrey was jumping up and down (with joy)." The dinner in our home solidified the relationship. Once again Margaret came through with her best under duress!

When our Founder, Dr. William Cameron Townsend (Uncle Cam), heard about the relationship, he asked me to invite the Secretary General to visit our work in Mexico. We were royally entertained and escorted (by plane) to an obscure mountain village to see a linguist-translator family at work.

Hospitality

We continued to fight these lies with hospitality, openness, and transparent honesty. When a new government administration came to power, we needed to start over. Again and again, we welcomed people of influence in the government and in the media to visit our center, learn about our operations, and find out the truth. As the director of our operations in Colombia, it was my job to handle challenges like this.

Since the Minister of Education was closest to the president, Uncle Cam and I invited him and his family to visit our center and stay in our home. During his visit, he met with local politicians, all of whom gave us a glowing endorsement. He saw our work. When he finished looking around, he looked at me with a puzzled expression on his face.

"Where is this opposition coming from?" the Minister of Education wondered.

When I told him, he nodded. He understood that the rumors about us had nothing to do with us. Instead, they were politically motivated by people on one side who wanted to drive Christianity out of the country and establish a Marxist state, and on the other side, those who wanted their brand of religion to be the only choice available in the nation.

In the morning, my wife and I offered him breakfast. At the end of our meal, I spoke to our guests.

"We've had our physical bread," I told them, "now it's time to share our spiritual bread, the Word of God." Then I turned to a Scripture passage and offered the Book to him so he could read aloud since he was much more fluent than I was in his native tongue.

As he rose from the table he said, "Thank you for asking me to read the Scriptures. It has been a long time since I've done that."

Then he smiled. "When will you next be in Bogotá? I want you to come to my office. I'll have something for you."

When Uncle Cam and I arrived in Bogotá, the Minister of Education thanked us again for being hospitable to him. Then he handed us a letter. That letter, which could only have been written with the president's consent, was filled with positive comments about Wycliffe's ministry. When he presented this letter, he said, "You may use this any way you wish."

Uncle Cam said, "We need to get this to the public." So he paid for the letter to be published in a quarter page ad in the three leading newspapers. At last, all over the country, people could read the truth. The Lord used that letter to continue to turn the tide in our favor.

Sometime later, my assistant and I were summoned to the same office of the Interior Minister who had given us the news that we would have to leave the country. This time the meeting was quite cordial. "I've just been talking to the President and he has decided to renew your contract. You can start working with my attorneys next week to begin the process," he said. I've often thought that this is just like the stories in the Old Testament where God's people were in an impossible situation, and He rescued them in an unusual way. It's good to know the God of the impossible. He's always there when we need Him.

No takers

But our enemies were not deterred. They kept looking for ways to get us removed. However, when the Minister of the Interior contacted Marxist university professors who were antagonistic to our work, he made an interesting discovery.

"We want their linguistic files," the university professors said. "Since you're kicking them out of the country, pack up their files and send them out to our universities."

But the Minister of the Interior replied, "No. If you are going to take over their work, you are going to go out into the jungle and live with the people, just like these people have been doing."

There weren't any takers.

Agricultural training

On another occasion, the Vice Minister of the Interior said to me, "You're under investigation. We're investigating every mission agency in Colombia, because we're not sure what they're doing."

Again, the Lord directed us to be honest and open. I brought him a report of what our mission had accomplished during the previous four years.

He started paging through it, and then suddenly he stopped. "Whoa! This is really important," he said, as he noticed we had awarded over a thousand diplomas in agricultural courses to Indian people during those four years.

Months later, I met with him again. He brought out my report and told me, "This is really important. You can't imagine how many times your opponents come here, sit in the same seat you're sitting in, lean over and say to me, 'When are you going to get rid of the gringos?' I get out this report, and I turn to this page and show them that you awarded over a thousand diplomas to Indians in the last four years. Then I ask them, 'How many diplomas have you awarded?'

"They slink out of my office with their tails between their legs."

Then he said to me, "If missions have to leave Colombia, yours will be the last to leave, because you don't just come here to save souls, but you care for the practical needs of our people."

Hostile journalist makes an unexpected discovery

We used the same open-door policy to deal with the journalist who reported that we were flying uranium and building missile silos. We picked him up, and flew him in our plane to Lomalinda. After a tour, he came to my office.

I was ready to field some tough questions, but he didn't give me any. Instead, he offered an apology. "I have to apologize," he said to me. "I've been smearing your reputation without knowing the truth about your work. Today, I've seen it, and I assure you that my attitude is changing. When I go back, I'm going to write the truth."

He did exactly that. He visited several times to gather material, and he wrote a wonderful series of articles in the newspaper. On one of these visits, he brought his wife and his mother-in-law. They had a meal in our home. One of our Colombian employees, who had just been led to the Lord, witnessed to the journalist's mother-in-law and led her to Christ!

This newspaper reporter, his wife, and his mother-in-law listened sympathetically to the Scriptures as we read them at the dining table. Shortly after that visit, he was killed in an automobile accident.

You never know when you may touch someone's life just before he steps into eternity.

Military investigation

One Saturday morning, as I was starting to leave on an errand, a helicopter flew over and landed at our center.

I turned around, and discovered that the helicopter was filled with top military and civilian officials, including two generals and a colonel. About that time a Colombian Navy truck drove up with a crew of frogmen. The general asked if he could meet with my administrators and me. So his party went up to my office. We met around a big table, and he opened his sealed orders. He said, "We are here to investigate your work."

I said, "Our doors are open. Do what you want."

So he sent his Signal Corps officers to look over our radio communications, and his Air Force people to check out our aviation program. An anthropologist reviewed our linguistics files.

The main party stayed through the morning. We prepared lunch for them. And then they conducted interrogations throughout the afternoon. The helicopter took off just in time to return to Bogotá before nightfall.

But they left a colonel in charge of intelligence to continue the investigation for another week, in case they'd missed anything.

His first day on a tour of the center, he was taken to the missionary kids' school. When he arrived at Anita's classroom, the teacher asked the students to sing the Colombian National Anthem that they had previously memorized. Anita said the colonel was moved to tears. "Why would the children learn our national anthem?" he inquired. "We love Colombia. It's our adopted country. This is one way we honor Colombia," was the answer.

During that week, our Colombian employee led the colonel to faith.

Then the colonel left. So they assigned a captain to replace him. And that man received the Lord. They replaced him with a lieutenant for another week. He also was sympathetic to the Gospel.

Finally, after three weeks they withdrew everyone. We missed the opportunity to convert the entire military!

Meanwhile, the frogmen were examining the lake. They were equipped with instruments to measure radioactivity. They stayed for ten days to see if the lake contained any uranium!

The captain of the Navy frogmen celebrated his birthday during their stay. We invited them all over for a birthday party at our house. My wife, Margaret, baked a cake in the form of a Colombian ship; she even put a little Colombian flag on a toothpick. We entertained these men, and they became good friends.

When they left, the commander of the frogmen apologized to me. He said, "You know, we have really bothered you people by having been here. I want to apologize, and explain that we were just following orders."

"No," I said, "we are happy that you came here so that you could check this whole thing out, and give an accurate report back to your government."

He smiled, "You know, we only found one thing here."

That surprised me. "What did you find?" I asked.

He said, "The only thing we found was *la presencia de Dios*—the presence of God."

For me, that was a crowning moment of our ministry in Colombia.

About this time, the journalist I mentioned was writing his series of articles. When I told him about this incident, he wrote an article in the newspaper called *"La Presencia de Dios"*—the Presence of God. As a result, the whole country learned that if you go to the mission center in Lomalinda, you will find the presence of God.

Some people will never experience the presence of God, until they come into contact with you or me. Our work of translating the Bible in Colombia was centered on one purpose: to bring the presence of God to the people of that nation.

Our enemies meant all of this opposition for evil, but just as God did for Joseph in Egypt, God turned it around for good.

Behind the scenes with Uncle Cam

1971-1976

When I was the newly appointed Superintendent of Aviation of the Colombia Branch, Uncle Cam used to take me to downtown Bogotá to visit government offices. We would visit officials all morning, then take a taxi to the guest house for lunch. Walking the streets at an elevation of 8,500 feet at his advanced age had to be tiring. But, instead of relaxing, he would read the New Testament to the taxi drivers and then dicker with them over the price, trying to get them to include the New Testament as part of the cost of the ride. I wonder how many Bogotá taxi drivers will be in heaven as a result of Uncle Cam's witness? And it was great training in Government Relations for a young pilot who would later be Field Director and need the experience and mentoring Uncle Cam gave me.

Cuauhtémoc was the son of Mexican President Lázaro Cárdenas (1934-40), the president who visited Uncle Cam in his Aztec village. When the president saw the linguistic and community development work of Uncle Cam and his wife, he invited him to bring more linguists to Mexico. Cuauhtémoc had been mayor of Mexico City and presidential candidate. He was a senator when he visited us in Colombia in 1971.

The new officials in the Colombian government needed more convincing evidence that our mission was a good thing for the country of Colombia.

Thanks to Uncle Cam, Cuauhtémoc arrived as our guest. His visit coincided with the new Colombian government administration. Cuauhtémoc visited our Lomalinda Center, met our mission members, and got a feel for our work in Colombia. We invited a host of important new government officials for dinner at the "Club Militar" in Bogotá. They all came to meet Cuauhtémoc. He gave a stirring speech about the valuable work our mission had done in Mexico. It was quite an evening. Margaret was elegantly dressed, and I wore a tuxedo, as part of the appropriate host attire.

Immediately after dinner, a new government official came to me and apologized. He said that he had talked badly about our mission to the new president, based on rumors and lies he had heard. He committed himself to go back to the president and correct this erroneous information. Both he and Dr. Vera, among others, became good friends that night. Others included the former Ministro de Gobierno and his wife. He had recently become the first president of our newly formed "patronato" (sponsors), but without really knowing a lot about us.

Dr. Vera became cooperative in signing papers for us, such as visa requests and importation documents. He visited Lomalinda, and eventually accepted Uncle Cam's invitation to Mexico. The following year, Dr. Vera and I visited the Mexico Branch, where Bob Goerz and the team made that trip a memorable one, arranging for us to visit the southern state of Chiapas, Mayan ruins, and a village where linguists were working.

Dr. Vera later visited in our home at Lomalinda. At breakfast, Margaret brought the Spanish New Testament and I turned to a passage about the peace of God, explaining that it was our custom to read the Scriptures as a family, partaking of spiritual food after the physical was consumed. Dr. Vera read in eloquent Spanish, and as he got to the "peace of God" passage, he stopped and addressed the official across from him at the table.

"This is what we need. We are at war inside. These people have peace," he said, as he pointed to our end of the table. After he completed the reading, we talked for about forty-five minutes about how we obtain the peace of God. Uncle Cam taught us to witness by reading the Word to visiting officials. It sure paid off in this instance.

In 1972, when our mission celebrated ten years since the signing of the contract, Dr. Vera requested and received an audience for us with the president. He personally accompanied several of us mission leaders and made sure the president signed a letter thanking our mission for our years of service to the country.

Wonderful hostess

Margaret was a great hostess. As Field Director, I was gone so often, traveling to Bogotá for government relations contacts and to Panama where personnel and programs were also my responsibility. As a result, I often didn't see the work she did and only learned about it later. Undeterred by the prestige of our guests nor by sheer numbers at times, she prepared delicious meals that pleased our guests and cleaned up afterward. She wrote home in February, 1973, that she had prepared and served 128 guest meals during January and 113 in February. She also organized the Valentine banquet for the missionaries at Lomalinda. She wrote, "It turned out very well, but I can't claim any glory for it, as the Lord brought organization out of what appeared to be pure chaos." In addition, she prepared refreshments for 30 maids who came to our home each week for Bible study, plus goodies for the weekly Pioneer Girls meetings. She had two receptions, one for *only* 30 people and another for 100 guests in the library up the hill. September, 1974, she wrote about preparing and serving 98 guest meals in our home in 16 days. What a wonderful ministry partner and wife she was, trusting the Lord for outcomes sometimes unpredictable, but ultimately good.

His Faithfulness Reaches to the Skies

In our newsletter covering 1974 events, Margaret wrote this summary:

- Guest meals: 1,000 (actual count)
- Guest nights: 239 (in our home)
- Forrey away from home: 40 nights
- Snacks: 1,300 (estimated)

In addition she stitched eleven aprons for the center dining room workers, sewed a friend's dress, and made a dress and matching panties for daughter Arlene. This occurred during the dry season when daily temperatures reached 100 degrees, and she worked without air conditioning and no dishwasher, and sometimes without the help of a maid. Many nights the temperature was in the 80s or 90s. Marvelous hostess and seamstress she was!

Forrest Zander

Chapter 6

RETURNING HOME

The road back home

1979+

In 1979 we returned to the USA for furlough. Our plan was to obtain additional education and return to Colombia. But the Lord had a different plan. Family needs arose that kept us in the States. In addition, as the director of the largest foreign organization in Colombia, I would have been a target in the wave of kidnappings of foreigners that spread across that nation in the 1980s.

During this time we dealt with a whole new set of pressures. My dad suffered a massive stroke and required nursing home care. Margaret fell and broke her ankle. Our son, Alby, injured his knee playing high school football and needed arthroscopic surgery. Then my dad experienced heart problems and had to be hospitalized. At the same time, my mom was in a car accident and suffered a heart attack. Then daughter Arlene called from the University of Illinois and told me that her financial aid was being canceled for that semester. I was busy directing Wycliffe's regional office in West Chicago, Illinois. I was training a new assistant, and things were going slower than he wanted. On top of all of this, we were very low on support. Wycliffe encouraged me to get out every weekend to speak in churches with the hope of raising our level of support. I was speaking every Sunday and sometimes on Wednesday nights.

This was beginning to feel like the first couple chapters of Job. If these things could be measured on a scale, the amount of stress at that time was close to the point where I felt like I was about to have a nervous breakdown. But I turned to the Psalms, just as I had done in Colombia. I chose to cast my cares, one by one, on the Lord. And God was faithful to bring peace and encouragement.

A window into Margaret's heart

1983

Our 25th wedding anniversary was fast approaching. Thoroughly bewildered at the thought of buying a gift for my wonderful wife Margaret, I decided the best approach was simply to ask. I might pick up a clue, and at least she'd know I hadn't forgotten!

"What should I get you for our anniversary?"

She replied, "I won't tell you. You'll laugh."

"No," I said, "I really want to know."

Avid Cubs fan that she was, she confided, "I want to go to Wrigley Field and see the Cubs play."

"OK," I said, "You've got it."

I purchased two tickets for September 27, almost behind home plate, just to the first base side and high enough to see the whole field. It was a good game with the Cubs leading 4-3 in the top of the ninth. Their fine closer was on the mound with two outs and two men on base, a real thriller.

At that high point in the game, I looked over at Margaret, and she was sharing her faith with the gentleman in the next seat! I could hardly believe it, but this was my Margaret, more interested in eternal things than a ball game. Maybe I had checked my faith at the entrance gate, looking forward to an entertaining afternoon. Margaret was on duty for God! And the Cubs went on to win the game, just as she did. Over the years, in admiration I watched her ask person after person, "Do you have Jesus in your heart?" By now, in heaven she's met some of them who responded to her question as the Holy Spirit used her to touch their hearts.

Fishing for men

2006

Margaret and I were on vacation in Wisconsin. It was early morning. The tiny inlet off the main lake was a popular fishing spot that attracted several regulars. I often fished there, but this morning I encountered something I didn't expect: a man, obviously stoned, was cussing loudly at me and becoming violent. I thought he was going to throw me in the lake. I was quite vulnerable, at the steep edge of the inlet with the angry man between me and a way of escape.

His Faithfulness Reaches to the Skies

I guess sharing with him about the Lord set him off.

"I am an attorney, but make most of my money as a garage fighter. I make $400 just for showing up. If I win, I get more," he boasted.

I noticed the wounds on his face from that last fight. It must have been recent. Perhaps the alcohol eased the pain of the wounds and the headache he probably had.

I had tried to share my faith with him as I hoped to do with at least one fisherman each morning. Most were polite and listened. One made it clear that there were two subjects he didn't discuss, religion and politics. I did get his name and pray for him to this day.

But this near violent episode made sharing my faith with this man unforgettable. As I listened to his rants, the garage fighter backed off enough for me to gather my fishing gear and head for my car. I added the attorney to my list and pray regularly for him. It will be interesting to find out some day how the Lord has worked in his life. I hope he doesn't get killed in a garage fight.

During another morning, a young man on a riding mower stopped to see how I was doing with the fishing. Fishing wasn't going well, so we started to talk. He mentioned that his name was Chris and that he was on community service for six months, working off his sentence for a misdemeanor. When I mentioned the Lord, he shared how his life had gotten off track. His sentencing had caused him to commit his life to God, and he hoped to continue in fellowship with the Lord. However, he confided that the old life with its temptations was drawing him back. I sensed the Lord had brought him to me. I put my arm around Chris as he sat on the mower. I prayed for him, for strength to endure, and for his future service. It was a sweet moment for both of us. I was encouraged, and I believe Chris was, too.

Cancer

2002

"You have prostate cancer," the urologist told me on August 16, 2002. We had suspected as much because my PSA level had jumped from 2.5 in the fall to 7.5 the following summer. A biopsy confirmed the diagnosis.

We went over the various options for treatment. If I were any older and my life expectancy around ten years, he would have recommended less invasive but less effective treatment. The best option for a "younger" person like myself was surgery to remove the prostate and eliminate the possibility of any return of the cancer. Since the type of cancer was in the mid-aggressive range, time was an important factor. We scheduled surgery for September 17.

Margaret and I went home stunned and concerned.

Once again, we turned to the Lord and found comfort in Psalm 91:14-16 NIV: "'Because he loves me,' says the Lord, 'I will rescue him; I will protect him, for he acknowledges my name. He will call upon me, and I will answer him; I will be with him in trouble, I will deliver him and honor him. With long life will I satisfy him, and show him my salvation.'"

His Faithfulness Reaches to the Skies

I told the surgeon that hundreds of people would be praying for him, and I know they were. Surgery was successful. The first few days after surgery were painful, but God gave me a complete recovery with no recurrence of the cancer.

Although this experience was scary, and recovery was painful, God's grace was on every part of it. The family of God rallied around us with prayer, cards, emails, and phone calls, and the love of God was evident in every one.

While I was recovering, before I knew I was cancer free, I wrote this poem, entitled "Jesus." It has since become my confession of faith.

Jesus

Jesus, you are my Savior.
Jesus, you are my Lord,
Jesus, I love you dearly.
Jesus, I love your Word.

Jesus, you are Creator
Of the ends of the earth.
Yet in humblest surroundings
You came by virgin birth.

Jesus, you came as the God-man
Jesus, you came to die.
Jesus, you did your Father's will.
You suffered for such as I.

Jesus, your cross was really mine.
You took this sinner's place.
Jesus, I give you my heartfelt thanks.
You died for the human race.

Jesus, the grave could not hold you.
You rose from that tomb of stone.
Jesus, you are coming again.
Soon you'll sit on your Throne.

Jesus, I give you the years that remain.
Jesus, I give you my all.
Jesus, I promise to serve you
Until I hear your call.

Lessons from Old Testament kings

The eyes of the Lord are looking at me.
He longs that I fully committed would be.
When I am with Him, He is with me.
Be strong, don't give up, and rewarded I'll be.

The eyes of the Lord are looking at me.
If I forsake Him, forsaken I'll be,
But when I repent and seek Him again,
His grace restores me to where I had been.

Sometimes I am tempted to follow my whim,
To depend on my wisdom and not follow Him.
But then I remember the lessons from Kings,
And return to the Lord for the blessing He brings.

His Faithfulness Reaches to the Skies

The lessons are clear from the life of the king,
Who either forsook God or to Him did cling.
"Oh, Lord, in your love, please help me to be
A wise, humble child, the pathway to see."

Still seeking the lost

2003

Margaret and I were babysitting grandchildren, Zach (5) and Matti (3), while their parents were out for the evening. After a playtime on the floor, Matti was tucked in bed. I was getting Zach ready for bed, but he asked if he could read books for a little while. I told him okay and that I would return and tuck him in. When I returned, the Holy Spirit moved my heart to ask Zach if he had asked Jesus into his life.

I was hesitant, but knew I had to be obedient to His leading.

Zach said, "When you were little like me, did you do that?"

"Yes," I said.

Then Zach said, "When Daddy was little like me, did you help him do that?

"Yes," I said.

"Then I want to do that," Zach said. And I had the joy of leading my grandson to the Savior.

As I tucked him in, he asked that I awaken him when his daddy and mommy got home. I promised to do that. He wanted to tell them about his experience. Of course, Alby and Lorri were delighted as was Margaret when I told her.

The next day, Zach told Matti that he had asked Jesus into his life and told her that she should do it, too. So Zach led his little sister to Jesus when less than a day had passed.

Several years later Margaret and I were invited to a baptismal service in their church. What a delightful experience to be present as Zach and Matti shared their faith and Alby baptized his two oldest children.

Margaret's passing

2012-2013

After our annual physical exams with our family internist in December 2012, we were pronounced in good health. By the end of January, however, Margaret was experiencing some unusual symptoms. The internist ordered a CT scan to determine if any problems existed. The results: see an oncologist. There appears to be something serious. Anita, Arlene, and Alby were present with Margaret and me when he gave us the alarming results: large tumors on the liver and the pancreas, with other areas also affected. Biopsies confirmed the cancer had spread, was inoperable and untreatable, and that Margaret had just weeks to live.

She went to be with Jesus on April 26, 2013. The visitation and memorial service were celebrations of a life of loving service for the Lord, faithfully lived, and mostly spent working on behalf of Bible translation. To have been married to this beautiful woman, Margaret, someone who loved the Lord and walked with Him, who prayed and interceded for so many friends and missionaries, and was my ministry partner for so many years, has been a wonderful experience.

But what about now? How could I continue without that faithful encouraging wife by my side?

Forrest & Margaret Zander

Forrest Zander

Anita's letter to her mom

May 2, 2013

Dear Mom,

The moment of truth has come—it's time to put on paper this love letter of thanks that I've been writing in my head for weeks. Of course I am deeply sad and will miss you terribly, but I am so glad we had a chance to say good-bye and that you are no longer suffering. Our last words were a friendly argument about which of us is the best mom—a lovely memory.

Here are a few of the things for which I am thankful.

Thank you for having me. The courage this took so soon after losing your first child as an infant is hard for me to fathom. Thinking about you meeting him again now brings tears of joy. You went on to give me the best childhood you possibly could, including many good things that you did not have or experience growing up. We always knew how important we were to you and Dad. You also raised us to be independent when the time came, so we will be all right without you.

Thank you for raising me to have faith in God. Every day I remember Bible stories you read, hymns we sang, and Bible verses you helped me memorize. My favorite is Psalm 139 that Matti read today.

I'm thankful for the siblings you gave me. Well, I'm thankful most of the time (just kidding) and now more than ever. Trying to do what was best for you while honoring your wishes about the care you received during your last illness brought the three of us and Dad closer as a family—a joy in the midst of our sadness.

I got the message from you to "do something right or not at all." Mostly I choose to do it right. Arlene and I have laughed that we choose not to clean house at all because we can't do it right. You once said you must not have taught us well when actually you set the standard so high that we just go with not doing it at all. Ha ha. Don't worry—when it comes to personal appearance, we do it right, thanks to you.

While I don't share your passion for the arts of homemaking, I appreciate them because of you. I married someone who makes sure we eat well and is a host with the most. Arlene and Alby have all that and the rest of the homemaking arts covered!

I seem to have also inherited your talents for perfectionism and procrastination. While I've gotten over the drive for perfection, I can take procrastination to a whole new level! Please notice that I am writing this two whole days before the service so that's an improvement. Nora is carrying on our fine tradition, too.

You taught by example the joy, privilege and responsibility of service. This is a core value for all three of us. Seeing that Nora got the same message is an ongoing source of pride and joy for me. In response to an article written recently by a dear friend and co-worker about my service experiences, you told me that you were proud to have me as a daughter. I am proud to be your daughter.

If a measure of a mother's success is reflected in whom her children choose to spend their lives with and how her grandchildren are raised, you did great. Arlene, Alby and I have chosen well and are off to a great start in raising our families. The longer I am married, the more blessed I am, and I could not be more proud of Nora Margaret. A huge thank you to you and Dad and to Tim's parents for showing us how to be good parents. I really wish we hadn't lost both you and Tim's mom so close together.

Your humility often extended to deflecting compliments you received. When you arrived in heaven and Jesus said, "Well done!" I know you finally believed it. No, you weren't perfect, but that is what grace is for. I hope you are enjoying all the dessert you want, because you can't "just have a bite of Dad's" for awhile yet.

Love you infinity!

Anita

A letter to family and friends

In the fall of 2013, I wrote the following letter which tells how my questions were answered:

I want to thank you for your wonderful encouragement and prayer during those difficult days when my beloved Margaret passed away. You were there for me and my family when we needed you most. Now I want you to REJOICE with me in a very wonderful blessing.

During those dark, dismal, difficult, and painful days following the home-going of my beloved Margaret, I prayed to the Lord, reminding Him that in dark and difficult events in our family history, He had shown Himself faithful, with the ability to turn a bad situation into one of light, hope, and blessing. I asked Him to do that for me again.

After the visitation and memorial service, daughter Arlene and family invited me to travel to visit them in Wisconsin. She suggested I get out of the house and away from the painful memories and stay with them, fishing, and spending time with grandsons, Charles and Colbey. One day as Arlene, Colbey, and I were at lunch, Colbey said, "Papa, now that Grandma Margaret is with Jesus, are you going to get married?" I wasn't ready for the question, and I'm not sure how I answered. Then he said to Arlene, "Mom, who can we hook him up with?"

Later, I pondered his question, and decided he needed an answer. So I thought about the characteristics of a person I might decide to marry. I told Colbey that first, I would look for a woman who is deeply spiritual, who loves the Lord her God with all her heart, soul, strength, and mind, and her neighbor as herself, even as Margaret did. Next, that she would be attractive and beautiful, as was Margaret. And lastly, that she would join me in ministry and travel with me to churches and project donor visits, to fill that empty seat beside me on trips. I wanted someone who would help me spread the word of the need for God's Word for those 1,967 languages still without any knowledge of God's love and Jesus' provision for their salvation. I shared this with Colbey and asked him to join me in praying for someone like this.

I asked my children how they would feel if I remarried and they were supportive, saying they trusted my judgment and wanted me to be happy. Also, I began to think of who might fit the above profile.

The Lord directed my thoughts to Wanda Jean Reid. She is a graduate of Moody Bible Institute, former missionary to Korea, with a BA in Education from Northern Illinois University, and with an MA degree in Christian Ministries from Wheaton Graduate School, where she met her husband, Rich. They were married and pastored churches in Minnesota, Montana, and Illinois. He was our pastor at Village Bible Church in Park Forest over twenty years ago before we moved to Winfield. They had the difficult experiences of losing a child at birth, and a 17-year-old son, who was killed while on a mission trip in Mexico. Then two years ago, her beloved husband Rich passed away after a difficult bout with cancer. Our experience of losing our baby in the jungles of Ecuador and my experience of Margaret's passing are somewhat parallel.

I decided to call Wanda. I asked if I could take her to dinner. My approach: We could be of mutual encouragement in our sadness and loss. She accepted, and I told her I would like to make it a very special evening, dress up, and go to an upscale restaurant. I brought a corsage and picked her up at her home in Park Forest. We had a delightful, enjoyable time communicating over a delicious dinner. On the way back, I took her through Glenwood and showed her the old Zander home where I grew up, the house on Birch Drive where we lived for 12 years after returning from Colombia, the church where I came to know the Lord, and the Sunday School building where I attended as a kid and later taught kids while a student at Moody.

I had already planned to drive to Wisconsin for another stint at Green Lake later that week. I asked Wanda if she would like to travel with me. She checked her schedule and was able to reschedule two conflicting dates.

We spent four wonderful days at the lake, praying, sharing Scripture and devotional thoughts, enjoying the beautiful scenery, and walking the wooded trails. We talked about every conceivable subject that couples beginning a relationship need to talk about. We found agreement in every area as the Lord began knitting our hearts together. By the end of the four days, we knew this relationship was from the Lord. Convinced of His leading, we committed to each other to be in an exclusive relationship. We felt that we had covered in four days what most couples would take six to eight months to work through.

The Children's Ministry staff at Appleton Alliance Church in Wisconsin had invited me to attend a special children's event the following Thursday, teaching the boys and girls how they could become missionaries. Wanda agreed to go with me. The staff had made a video of me telling pilot stories from South America and wanted the kids to meet the character in the video and see how missionaries can be pilots, computer specialists, teachers, nurses, etc. We set up a display of artifacts including an alligator head (with teeth), 16-foot boa constrictor snake skin, jungle blow gun, and a prayer card describing how kids can pray for a Bible-less language. It was loosely organized with kids coming and going, including some with parents. Wanda helped gather the kids in groups to our table where I demonstrated the snake skin, popped balloons with the blow gun, and gave each one a Bible-less peoples' prayer card.

After the event, Wanda and I returned to Green Lake for the night. Before retiring, and encouraged with how our relationship was blossoming, I got down on my knees, looked into her beautiful blue eyes, and proposed.

Oh, joy! Wanda said, "yes."

We have set the date for Sunday, October 13, 2013, at her church, Village Church of Dyer, Indiana, with her senior pastor officiating. Attending will be only immediate family: Wanda's parents, our siblings and their spouses, our children and their spouses, and my grandchildren. Son Alby will be my best man, and Wanda's daughter, Jeanine, will be her bridesmaid. After the ceremony, the 28 of us will celebrate at the same restaurant where we had our first date.

Since both of us had such wonderful first marriages, we are honoring our dearly departed spouses by marrying again.

As you ponder this story and the marvelous way that the Lord has answered my prayer, in a manner over and above what I could have thought or imagined, please thank Him for this abundant blessing, and pray that together Wanda and I will honor the Lord in a greater way than ever before.

Gratefully,

Forrest

Letter from Wanda

2014

Dear Anita, Arlene, and Alby,

As we begin a new year, I want to express to you how thankful I am for your acceptance of your dad's and my relationship. I am very cognizant of the fact that your first holiday season without your mother and all the special touches that she brought to your family gatherings has been a sad one for you. And that adds to my gratitude for the love you have expressed to me. Each of you has expressed it in specific ways that have been a great encouragement to me.

When Rich and I moved to Park Forest in 1990 and met your mom and dad, I could not in my wildest imagination have anticipated that your dad and I would each be widowed and would be blessed with an opportunity for a second happy marriage. **But God** (V. Raymond Edman wrote a book by that title) has done above and beyond what either of us could have asked for, and we are grateful.

I know that you are aware of it, but I want to assure you of it again—your dad is extremely proud of each of you, your spouses, and your children. Whether he is talking to me or to others, he speaks of you with great pride. And he credits your mom (second only to the Lord) with the special person that each of you has become, because his work responsibilities left much of the parenting to her. Know, also, that we pray for you and the members of your family daily. Before we get out of bed each morning, he leads us in prayer for each of you and your families.

I am confident that your dad loved your mom totally, and he did everything he could to demonstrate that love to her. It shows in the way he speaks of her. And now, I am blessed to be the recipient of that sacrificial, unconditional love that reflects to me the nature of God's love. It says a lot for the quality of your dad's character that he is able to adapt to a different woman and show love in a way that is meaningful to me, just as he did to your mom.

Thank you, again, for allowing me the privilege of loving your dad without it being marred by feelings of rejection from any of you. May God bless each of you richly for trusting your dad and the Lord enough to allow Him to bring us together in such an amazing way. May each of us always give the glory to Him alone.

With love,

Wanda

Colombia

God has done a wonderful work in Colombia. Since 1962, thirty-eight languages in Colombia have the entire New Testament. Each of these thirty-eight languages represents a separate people group. Each of these people groups might contain anywhere from 200 to over 100,000 people.

Sometimes people say, "Is it really worth it to spend the better part of a lifetime for 200 people?" But I reply, "How many pastors spend the better part of a lifetime pastoring a flock of 50 to 100 to 200 people? Investing our lives in the lives of other people is never a waste of time."

God's Word transforms lives, cultures, and nations. The Guambiano people grew poppies, a crop that made Colombia a major worldwide exporter of opium. But as Wycliffe missionaries, Tom and Judy Branks, with a team of Christians from their language group, translated the New Testament into the Guambiano language, people came to Christ. One of these Christians became governor of that area. He used his influence to encourage his people to burn their poppy fields and plant legitimate crops. The result? The Word of God succeeded where drug enforcement agencies often fail, and international drug traffic was stopped at its root.

The Word of God is still bearing fruit.

Looking ahead

Since Uncle Cam began his work in the 1930s, Wycliffe has translated the New Testament into over 1,000 languages. Translation is in process for about 2,200 languages right now (2015). 1,833 languages still need a translation. For the first time in the history of the church, the number of languages with translation-in-progress exceeds the number of languages needing Bible translation. Here is the progress in recent years since Vision 2025 that every language in the world that needs a Bible translation will have one in progress by 2025 has become Wycliffe's mission. Here's where we stand:

- **1999: 3,000 languages to go**
- **2005: 2,529 languages to go**
- **2015: 1,833 languages to go**
- **2025: 0 languages to go (goal)**

Forrest Zander

Orville Johnson translating the New Testament into the Secoya language of eastern Ecuador. Celestino, with the typical crown made from the feathers of colorful jungle birds, became the first Secoya believer and pastor.

My heart is warmed as I read of the transforming power of the Word of God in the heart languages of people around the world. As a result of Bible translation, people are evangelized; churches are planted and grow; indigenous people are discipled and rise up to become spiritual leaders in the emerging church. Missionaries work themselves out of a job, and move on to another assignment.

I currently serve as Wycliffe's Regional Director of Advancement and Minister-at-Large. My role is to raise financial and prayer support for these endeavors. Everywhere I go, I take the message, "You can be a vital part of this ministry, right where you are, by praying daily for a Bible-less people group." For those who take on the challenge of praying, Wycliffe provides resources and updates so they can pray intelligently. Visit www.wycliffe.org/prayer

To find helpful resources for your church missions program: shop.wycliffe.org

For helping children understand missions: www.wycliffe.org/resources/kids-activities

Even though I reached retirement age a long time ago, I plan to continue to serve as long as the Lord gives good health and a meaningful ministry. Moses, Joshua, and others kept on going; I hope to do the same.

Our family

Although our first child died as a baby, God graciously gave us three more children, who have given us eight grandchildren.

Anita, married to Tim Murphy, earned a master's degree in nursing and works as a Nurse Practitioner in the Chicago area.

Arlene, married to Randall Johnson, graduated with a degree in Aeronautical/Astronautical Engineering, and worked as an award-winning engineer for McDonnell Douglas.

Albert, married to Lorraine (Newton) holds a BA degree in Education/Exercise science and MA degrees in Urban Ministry and Educational Leadership. He teaches and coaches football and basketball in a public high school in suburban Chicago.

All three children continue to be active in missions ministry at home and abroad.

Forrest & Wanda with our four children

My eight grandchildren

Nora Margaret Murphy, Anna Marie "Anita" Zander Murphy, Timothy John Murphy.

Forrest Zander

Arlene & Randy Johnson, Charles, Colbey

Albert and Lorri Zander with their children, left to right, Matti, Benji, Leeya, Samson, and Zach

Forrest and Wanda Zander

About the authors

Forrest and his wife Margaret served with Wycliffe Bible Translators in South America for 20+ years, before returning to the States where he now serves as Associate Director of Advancement & Minister-at-Large, speaking in churches and other venues on behalf of Wycliffe. He holds a diploma in Missionary Aviation from Moody Bible Institute. He also holds a BA and MBA from Governor's State University. He has served on the Wycliffe Board of Directors and Moody Bible Institute Alumni Association Board of Directors (two years as Board President). He is currently on the Aramaic Bible Translation Board of Directors, where he served as Chairman for 18 years. In 1980, he received the Alumnus of the Year Award from Moody Bible Institute. In 1995, he was inducted into the Bloom Township High School Hall of Fame. Following Margaret's homegoing, he married Wanda Reid. The two of them have four adult children and eight grandchildren. Forrest and Wanda Zander live in suburban Chicago. Forrest can be contacted at forrest_zander@wycliffe.org. Visit www.wycliffe.org for more information.

Ghostwriter and author Dwight Clough lives in Sun Prairie, Wisconsin. To contact Dwight or learn more about his writing services, visit DwightClough.com. Learn about Dwight's books here: DwightClough.com/books2.

The glory goes to God

In 1980, I was honored as Moody Bible Institute's Alumnus of the Year. They give these awards to men and women, but the real credit belongs to God. He's the one who saved my life countless times. He is the one who worked in the hearts of government officials and others in Colombia, and opened their eyes to see and embrace the truth. With my Wycliffe colleagues, I have been blessed to be a small part of His great story.

Made in the USA
Middletown, DE
27 May 2016